The English DINKY BUS & COACH

A Personal Journey
& Dream of
Roger Bailey

Issue 1 August 2021

Printed by Flexpress Leicester

Copyright Roger Bailey Promotions

The right of Roger Bailey to be identified as the author of this work has been asserted by him in accordance with the copyrights, designs and patents act 1988.

All rights reserved. No part of this book may be printed or reproduced or utilised in any form or any electronic, mechanical or other means, now known or hereafter invented. Including photocopying and recording, or in any information storage or retrieval system, or used in presentations, without the author's permission.

Roger Bailey
August 2021

Thanks to:

- my parents, Maurine and Jim Bailey, who helped me to develop my love of buses from an early age
- Nigel McMillan who took many of the photographs over a long period of time, and whose work can be seen in earlier issues of Diecast Collector
- David Wallace for his help and support with photographs and information
- Henry Clarke for many of the drawings used and Mike Gorman for use of his 20th Century images of the Meccano factory in Liverpool in the 1950s.

Along this personal and long journey, many collectors have contributed information and the occasional photograph including W.Waugh, Norman Rusbridge, R.P.Fryer, Chris Pearson, Eric Diamond, Brian Nunn, James Stirling, David Brady, Nelson Twells, Michael Driver, Arnold Chave, Brian Hooper, Mike Forbes, Graham Bailey, Hugh MacKinnon, Vic Davey, Paul and Hilary Kennelly and the Time Machine in Coventry.

I want to thank you all, sadly some are no longer with us.

Special thanks to Pauline Venables for all her patience and many hours of work as the editor and designer of this book. She questioned and challenged me to look at things differently.
Without her this book might never have seen the light of day.

If you can add to this book then please email dinkybusesandcoaches@gmail.com

INDEX

Introduction	
Motor Bus	1
Tramcar	3
Double Deck Bus	4
Type 1 - pre war	4
Type 1 - post war	8
Type 2 (launch 1948)	12
Type 2 (re-introduced 1954)	15
Type 2 'Exide Batteries'	28
Type 2 - Cream livery	31
Type 3 (launch 1949)	33
Leyland Atlantean	41
Routemaster London Bus	50
Atlantean City Bus	61
Streamlined Bus	69
Single Deck Bus	74
Luxury Coach	78
Observation Coach	83
Duple Roadmaster Coach	88
BOAC Coach	97
Atlas Bus	100
Wayne School Bus	102
Continental Touring Coach	103
Vega Major Luxury Coach	105
Luxury Coach	109
Single Deck Bus	111
Planned but never produced	114

Dinky Copies

Diecast Copies	
Streamlined Bus	120
Luxury Coach	121
Observation Coach	123
Double Deck Bus	124
The Dinky Toys Collectors Association	125
Kits	126
The Morestone Bus	127
The Metosul Bus	129
Plastic Copies	
Luxury Coach	138
Double Deck Bus	139
Streamlined Bus	139
Duple Roadmaster Coach	140
Routemaster Bus	141
Wayne School Bus	143
Vega Major Luxury Coach	144
Leyland Atlantean	145
BOAC Coach	147
Single Deck Bus	148
Atlantean City Bus	149

Introduction - The English Dinky Bus and Coach

My journey with Dinky started when I was about 7 years old and given my first Dinky bus. The following year I inherited my uncle's toys which included 3 Dinky buses, which I still have but they've been repainted

On my regular visits to my grandmother there was always a new toy for me. Predominantly they would be Matchbox, but twice I was given a Dinky Leyland Atlantean from the early 1960s, which I still have.

For me the toyshops of the 1960s were magical places. I'd spend ages with my nose pressed up against the shop windows to better see their Dinky range. The Barnaby's store was spectacular at Christmas time with their 'Dinky Roadways Layout'. Shops in my home city often had old Dinky toys which were sometimes sold off cheap to make room for new stock.

Great memories.

For as long as I can remember I've been interested in finding out more about Dinkys. The book by Cecil Gibson on the history of Dinky Toys from 1934 to 1964 was certainly a good starting point. My copy is a first edition dated 1966. Other great sources of additional information include the List of Dinky 29C/290/291 variations as produced by P Cox and Pirate Models and later made available by John Gay. As is the history of the whole range by Mike and Sue Richardson first and second edition.

The Model Bus federation was formed in 1968 and I joined in 1969 at the age of 13. The Coventry Diecast Model Club started in 1975 and I was its 20th member. In the 1980s and 1990s, I was a member of the Maidenhead Static Model Club often attending their meetings and I went on several trips with them to toyfairs in Brussels and Germany. In 2003 the Dinky Toys Collectors Association was created and I was one of the first members.

During Meccano's production of Dinky Toys from 1934 to 1979, there were always buses and coaches in the range. They were often based on obscure real vehicles with a variety of castings and liveries.

As I gathered more knowledge and information I started producing articles for a variety of magazines, including Model Collector, Modellers World, Classic Toys, Collectors Gazette, and later for Diecast Collector. I've always dreamt of putting these many articles together into one book so that I could share my knowledge. Naturally over the years the content of these articles has been revised as new toys and information has surfaced. The Internet has certainly greatly enhanced this as collectors all over the world are now in touch.

I'm sure that there is a lot still out there that I don't know about. However I needed to produce my first book with my current knowledge. It's not an easy subject, as it has been difficult to confirm all the different variations in casting and livery. With limited records from the company itself and sometimes some flexibility on what came down the production line, variations continue to be found and new information discovered even in the 21st Century.

There has been a need to separate the variations between castings of each model, so the terms Type 1, Type 2 etc has been adopted on occasions.

This book has been over thirty years in the making.
It's been my personal journey to catalogue and list all the variations of the English Dinky buses and coaches throughout their production.
At last my dream has been realised, but who knows what there is still to be discovered.
Perhaps you can add more to this story?

Roger Bailey
August 2021

Here I can be seen playing with 2 of the Dinky buses inherited from my uncle.

Motor Bus

The AEC Q vehicles were revolutionary for the time with:
- full front *as opposed to half cabs*
- engine located under the stairs on the offside *as opposed to at the front*
- passenger entrance at the front or centre *as opposed to rear platform*
- stairs were behind the driver's cab *as opposed to the rear*

Its design matched the Art Deco style of the time. Perhaps too futuristic for the bus industry though as only 23 were produced with the last being in 1936. However AEC did have more success with their single decker variant.

In 1934 Dinky launched Motor Bus which was their first double decker toy.

It's believed to be based on the AEC Q's in service in Grimsby or possibly Wallasey because of the central entrance.

Production of the Dinky bus stopped in 1938 and they never produced their single decker version that they had planned.

The toy was initially catalogue number 29 but later changed to 29a.

The base livery was mid green, mid blue, maroon or red. The upper deck windows and roof were cream but sometimes believed to be white.

There was also a yellow/ silver variant.

Wheels were normally plated metal, but a few came with Bakelite.

Many carried adverts for 'MARMITE DEFINITELY DOES YOU GOOD'.

The 'Marmite' lettering was either red or silver and edged in black with the remainder of the advert being black.

Toys produced towards the end didn't have adverts but did have the Bakelite wheels.

Tramcar

The Tramcar appears to be based on a standard London County Council tram built for service in the London area. Which later became known as London Passenger Transport Board standard E1 series of trams.

The toy, catalogue number 27, was produced from 1934 to 1939 and was a single metal casting with no base plate.

Originally produced with split green plastic rollers, as used on the Dinky train sets. These were quickly replaced by small metal wheels held in place by crimpled axles.

The livery of the early toys had a lighter colour of cream on the lower and upper windows plus the roof and running gear. Upper and lower panels or just lower panels were painted a darker colour.

While later versions have the upper section in cream including the top deck windows, with mid green, orange, red, yellow, mid blue, light blue on the rest of the tram.

Later examples had adverts. The 'Ovaltine' lettering was in red edged in black with the remainder of the advert being black.

Double Deck Bus

This classic toy was in production from 1938 until 1963. Throughout its manufacture it remained basically the same toy but with a number of casting changes, though clearly showing signs of wear after so many years.

There were three basic types of casting for this toy and each had a different radiator plus other slight changes. For simplicity here they're called Types 1, 2 and 3. One of the challenges for the collector is that several moulds were being used and so there are many combinations to look for. Sometimes more than one type was being made at the same time as another, with the total number of variations claimed to be in excess of 70.

The catalogue number was 29c when released in 1938, but by 1954 it had been renumbered as 290, and the 'Exide' variant in 1959 had the catalogue number 291.

Type 1 - Pre-war 1938 to 1940
This toy is based on the AEC STL and was in service for London Transport. These were an AEC Regent with most of the bodies built by the London Passenger Transport Board (LPTB) at its Chiswick premises. Production lasted through most of the 1930's.

Its catalogue number was 29c. Initially it was manufactured with a short staircase but this was removed in late 1939. The model had ribbing added to the interior between the windows, three on each side.

A very distinctive feature was the cutaway wings on the front elevation and the plain wheel hubs. The axle was thin and not boxed-in around the front wheel arch. The wording on the chassis was revised in 1939 with a different typeface. These pre-war toys can be prone to metal fatigue, so watch out for cracks in the body of the bus. The impurities grow and often cause swelling.

The bottom section of the toy was painted in a variety of colours: red, light green, dark green, light blue, dark blue and maroon. *Orange has also been suggested, but there is limited evidence for this colour variation.* The upper section was invariably cream and earlier versions had a grey roof.

The advertisement for 'Dunlop Tyres' appeared on the toy.

They were only sold in tradeboxes of 6.

5

Pre-war examples showing all five liveries.

Photographs by D Wallace

It's been suggested that these carved wooden toys date back to the war years.

They have Dinky type 1 wheels!

There would have still been a stock of wheels at the Meccano factory, but normal toys were not at the time being produced.

Pre-war axle

Post-war axle

Type 1 - Post-war 1946 to early 1948

The toy reappeared in 1946.

The axle was thicker and boxed-in around the front wheel arch.

By 1947, the plain wheel hubs had been replaced by the inner-ring type.

The first livery of post-war production: red/grey, green/grey, green/cream and red/cream.

Small batches of the final castings in 1947 appeared in a two-tone green livery. The light green upper-deck paintwork is prone to flaking and so examples in mint condition are rare.

Two-tone green livery

There were no advertisements on the toy and the wheel hubs were always black.

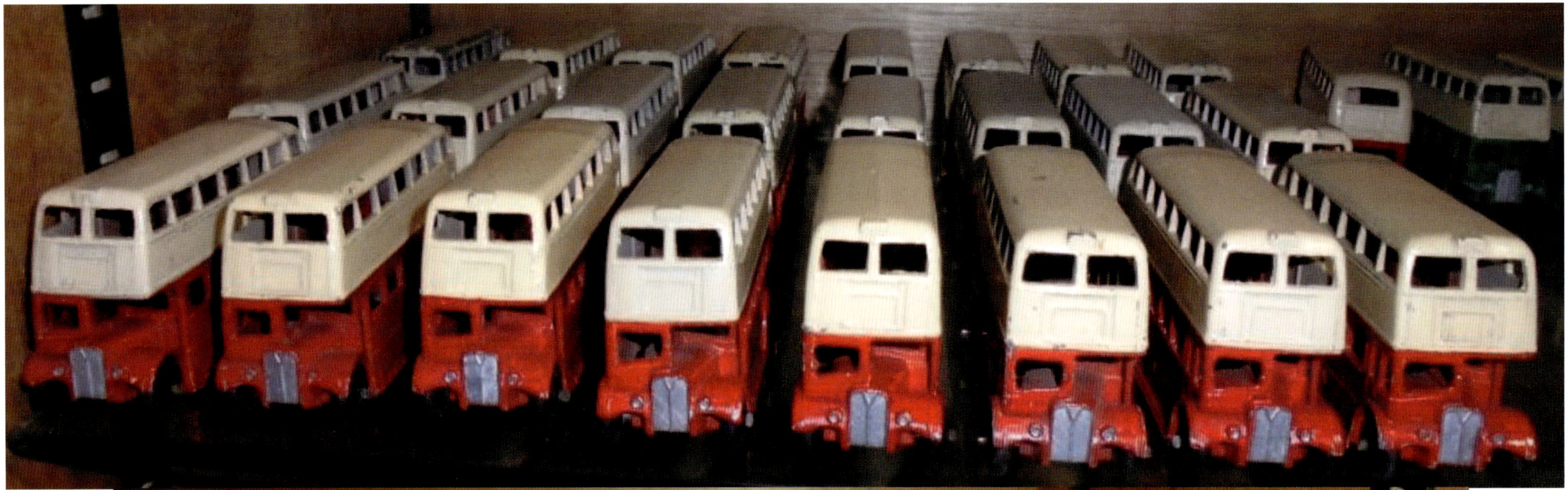

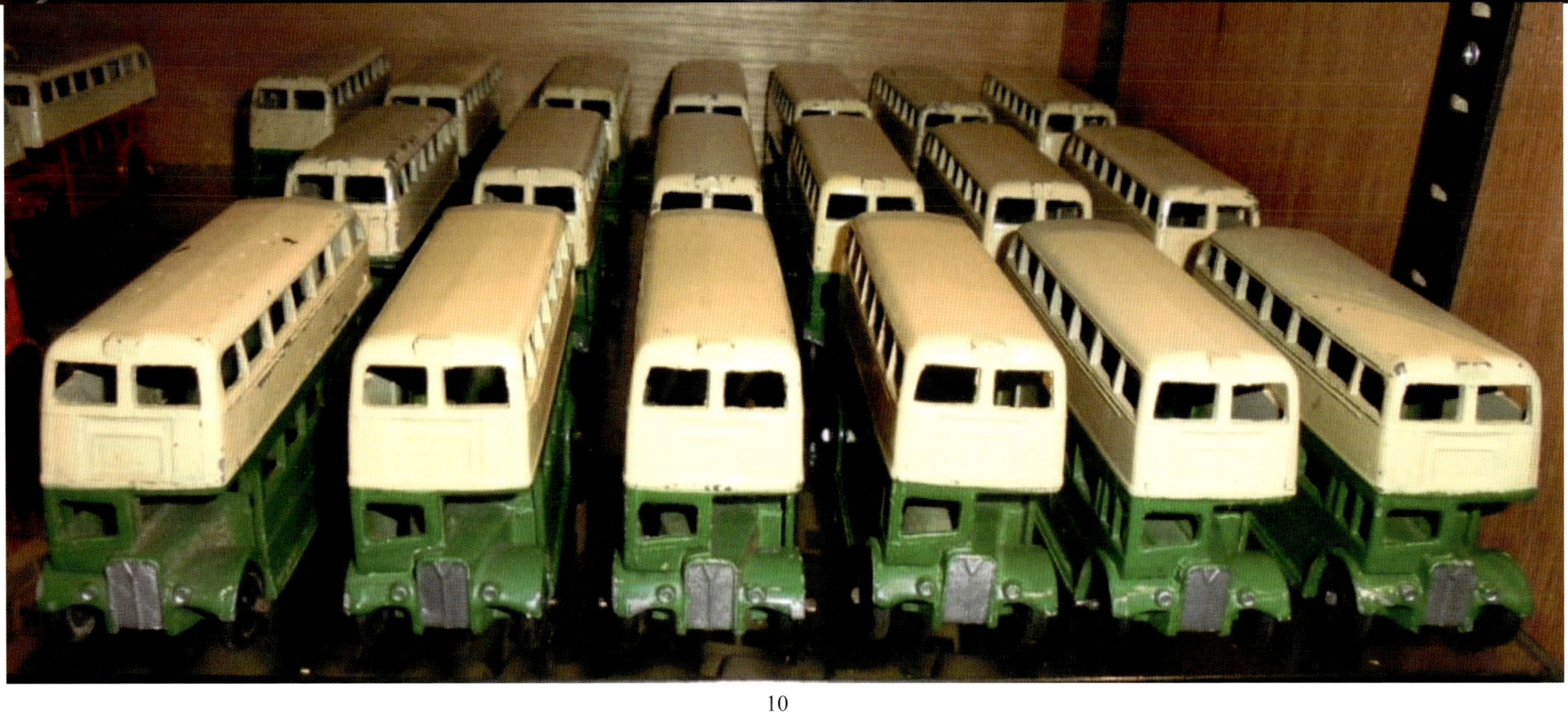

Type 2 (Catalogue numbers 29c and 290)

Type 2 is based on the Leyland STD (Titan PD1), with a roof-box, which is believed to be based on service vehicles delivered to London Transport in 1946.

The toy was unveiled in 1948.

It was re-issued in 1954 as the Leyland Titan, and continued in production until the end of the range in 1963.

In the first year a small number were produced with black wheel hubs. These were quickly replaced by coloured wheel hubs which corresponded with the livery of the lower deck of the bus so either red of green.

After the first year, a raised metal strip was added along the centre of the interior floor that ran between the entrance and the small hole in the centre.

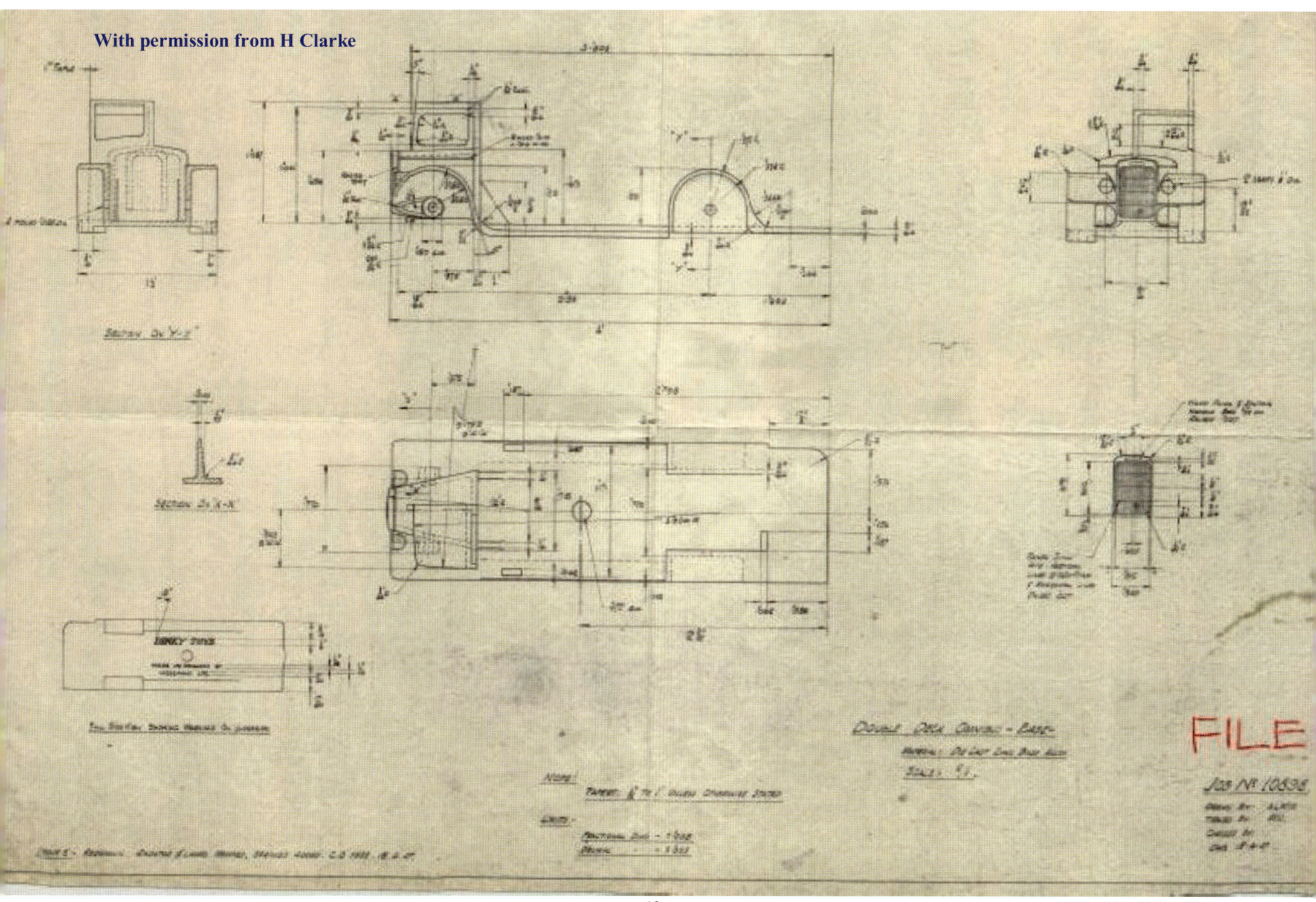

With permission from H Clarke

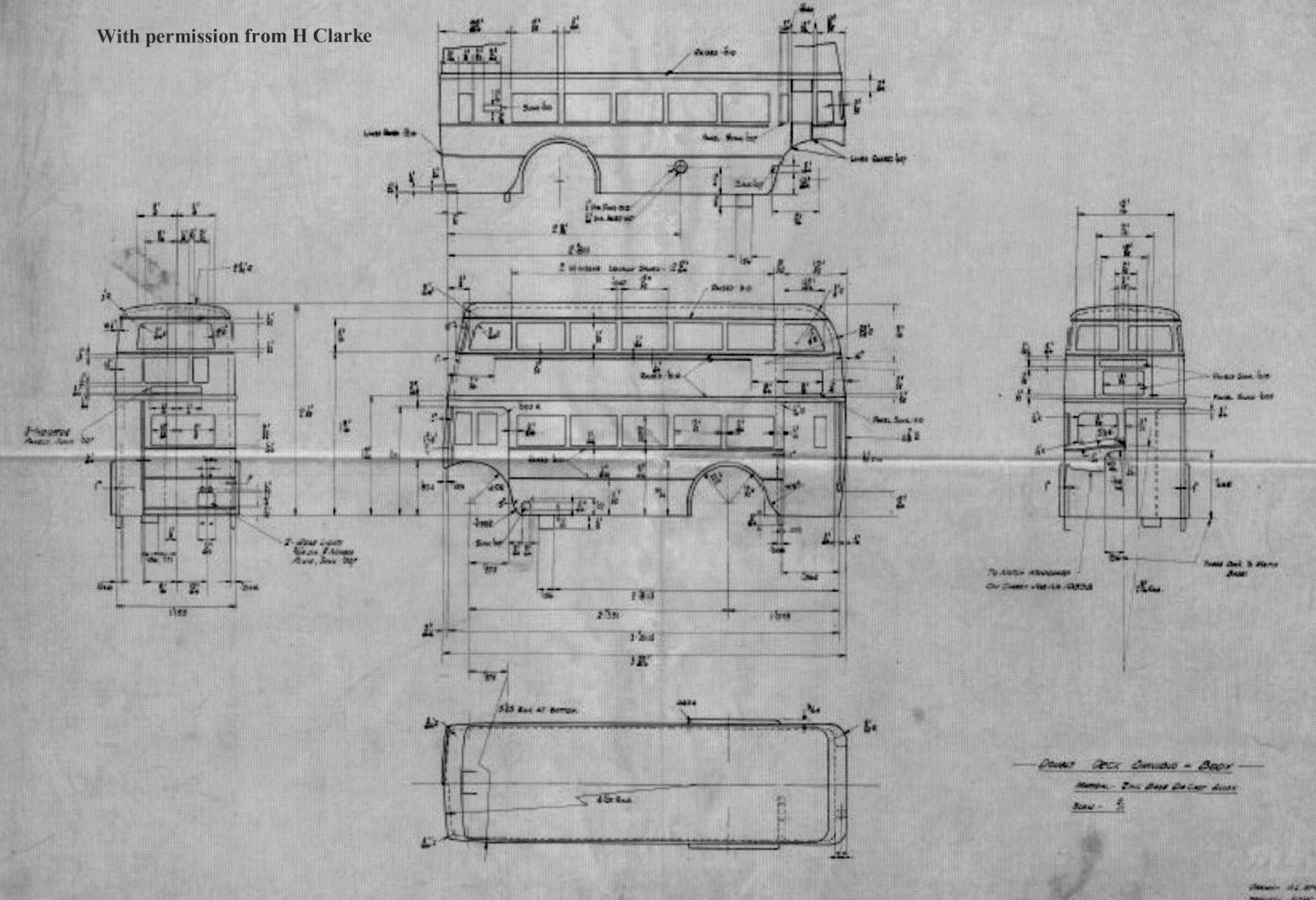

Type 2 - Leyland Titan - catalogue number 29c

Casting changes when type 2 was re-introduced in 1954:
- body redesigned and the original six ribs between the interior windows were spaced to correspond with every other window, making a total of five: two on the nearside and three on the offside
- pin-head axles
- larger side destination screen
- smaller rear destination screen
- larger rear top windows
- smaller rear lower windows
- smaller driver's window
- more upright rear profile
- smaller offside staircase window
- a more squared front nearside canopy
- side and front windows reshaped.

Within a year the hole in the middle of the chassis had been filled in and the raised metal strip inside was extended to the bulkhead. Advertisements were introduced.

By 1955/1956 casting changes: catalogue number 290 was embossed on chassis; the roof box was deleted, *possibly due to worn dies, but there are toys with a roof box and bearing the catalogue number of 290*. Within a couple of years the advert letters of 'Dunlop' were made thinner.

By no later than 1959 further casting changes: the indented rear stoplights and number plate were removed, catalogue number was removed from the chassis.

In 1960, the roof box was re-instated and the upper-deck front windows were enlarged.

In 1961, the upper-deck rear windows were enlarged and the letters of 'Dunlop' were changed from straight to slanted.

Type 2 toy seen from all angles

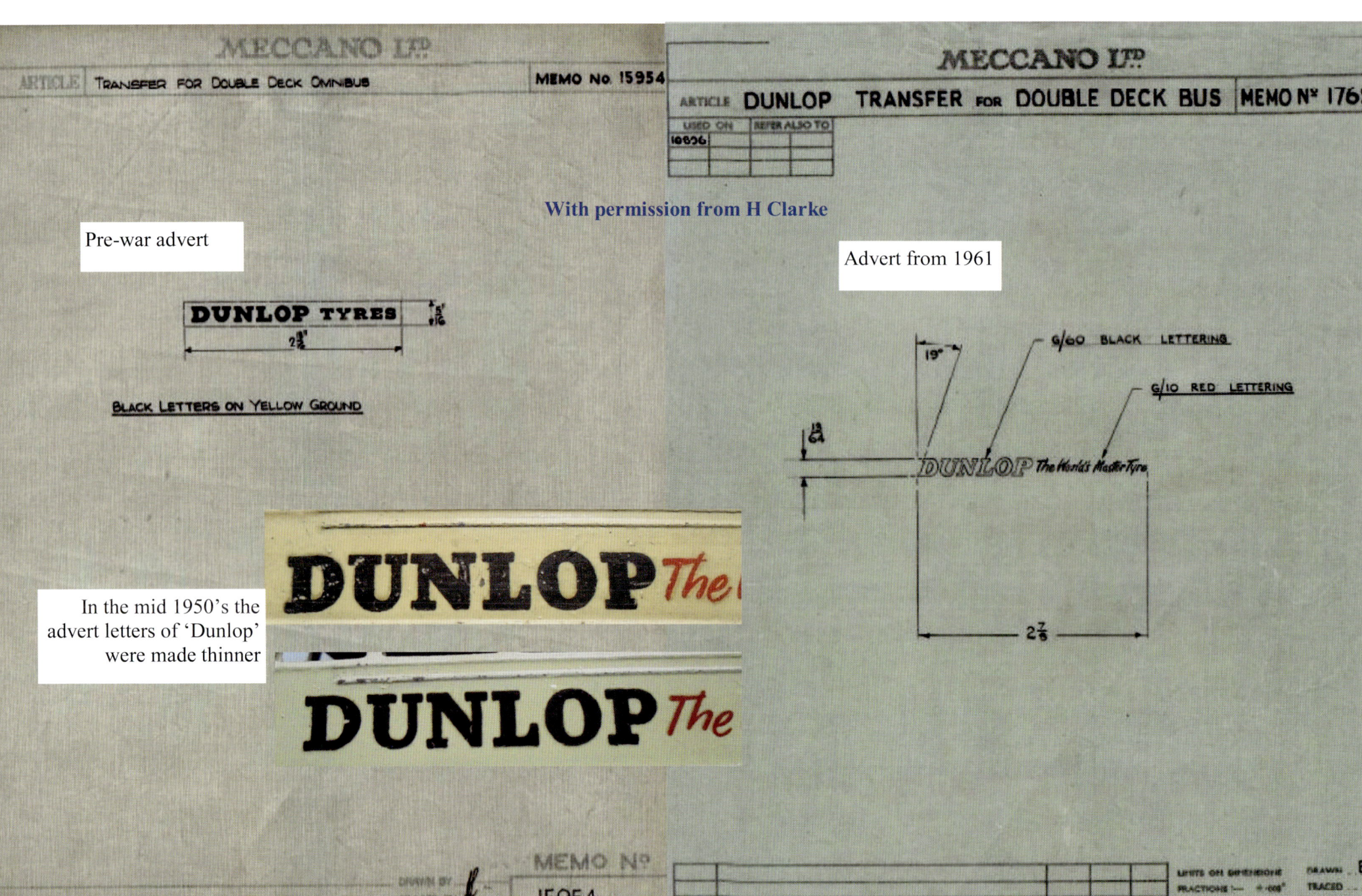

For the greater part of the production life of the toy the livery was either green/cream or red/cream. In 1961, a lighter green/cream livery was introduced, initially on a batch with cast wheels and black or white tyres, but subsequently on both the spun and plastic wheel variants.

However the standard green colour continued until well into 1962. The shade of red also varies over time. Quality control was an issue in later years and it is not unusual to see what is in fact a mint condition toy bearing paintbrush marks. There is evidence that touching up took place before some left the factory.

There have been some sightings of toys which are a little different from the normal production run for example with unpainted radiators.

'Dunlop' original straight lettering

'Dunlop' post 1961 sloping lettering

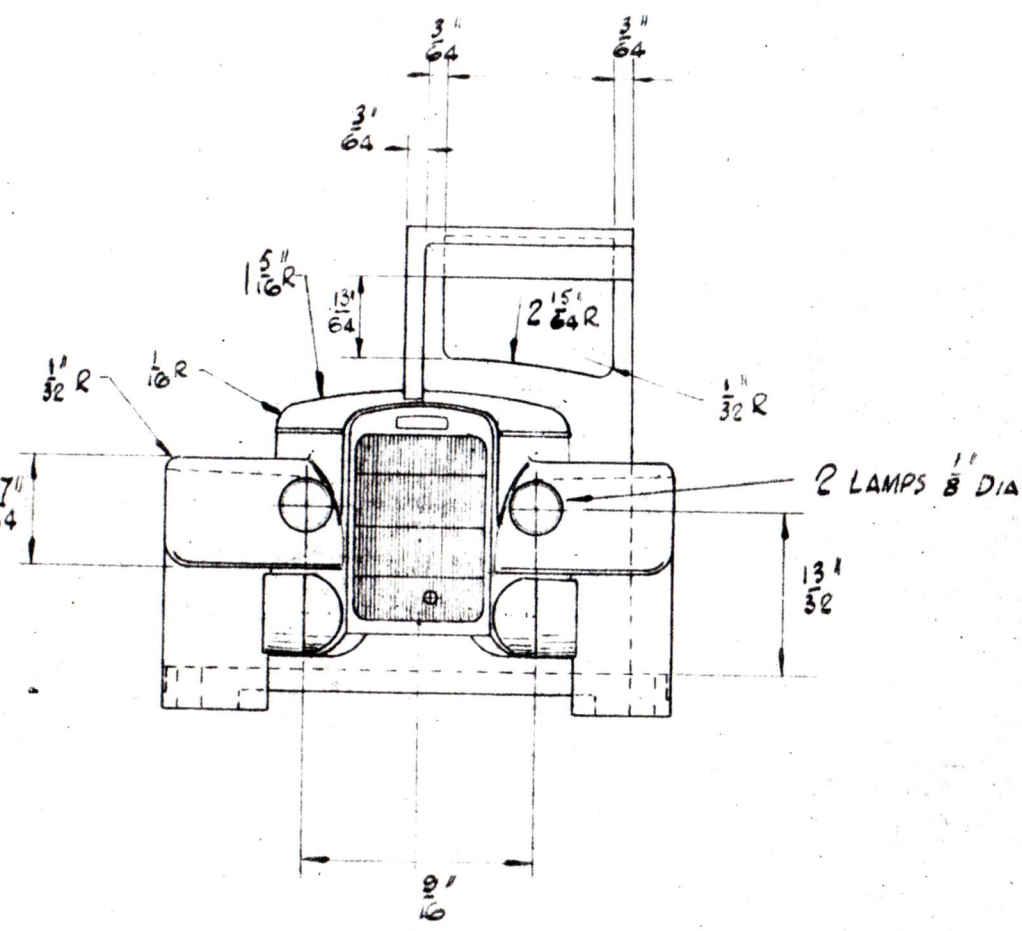

Photograph was taken in 1957 on the Meccano production line in Liverpool.
Copyright owned by www.20thcenturyimages.co.uk.

A variety of Type 2 through the ages

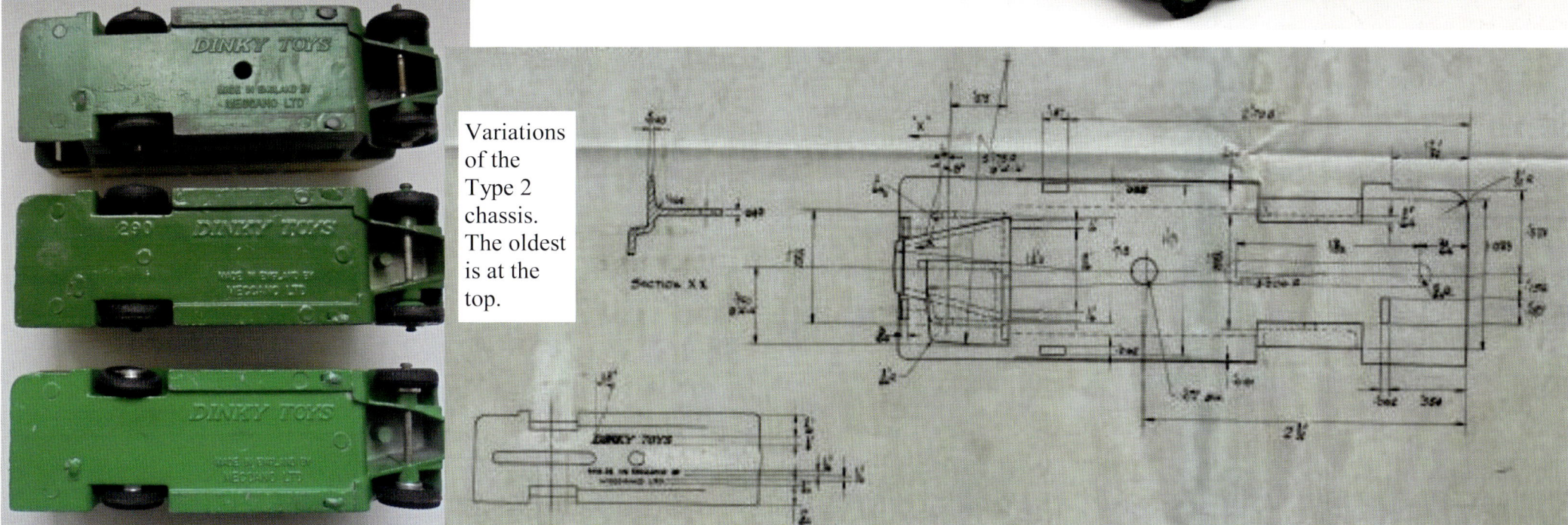

Variations of the Type 2 chassis. The oldest is at the top.

21

A rare example of a toy with light-green painted cast wheels.

Comparison between a 1950s and a much later Type 2 casting:

1. Older casting with well defined registration plate and rear stoplights, smaller upper deck front and back windows
2. Castings towards the end of production with larger upper deck front and back windows

During 1961/1962 the cast wheels were replaced by spun wheels.

A line-up of Type 2 showing all three wheel variants:
- cast
- plastic
- spun

During 1962/1963 the spun wheels were replaced by coloured plastic wheels.

Production of this toy ceased in 1963 yet stocks were still held in the factory until the early part of 1964 and they could be found for sale until the early 1970's.

Lighter green livery

Darker green livery

There is no obvious explanation for the different livery colourings but it highlights the challenges of trying to list all versions of this toy in chronological order.

Toys with and without the adverts, which happened on occasions.

Photograph was taken in 1957 on the Meccano production line in Liverpool.
Copyright owned by www.20thcenturyimages.co.uk.

'Exide Batteries' Type 2

The all-red bus with advertisements for 'Exide Batteries', with catalogue number 291, was to be the final version of this toy.

The first version appeared in 1959, initially with no roof box and smaller upper-deck front windows.

Some are said to be in red/cream and green/cream liveries with the advertisement along the sides.

Casting changes:
- in 1960, the roof box was re-introduced and the number 73 appeared on the front destination screen of some
- later in 1960 the upper-deck front window was enlarged
- in 1961 the upper-deck rear window was enlarged
- in 1961/1962 cast wheels replaced by spun wheels
- in 1962/1963 spun wheels replaced by coloured plastic wheels

There are many surprises accompanying this variant. It has been suggested that a small batch was produced, of the earlier version, for a special order but carrying London Transport fleet names. Others have been seen carrying yellow transfers on both sides for 'TyreBatt Ltd - Bath 5116', *probably simply added for local consumption, but nevertheless an interesting addition of authenticity and relevance to any collection.*

The catalogue number 291 never appeared on the chassis, but a few of the early examples carried the original catalogue number of 290.

A very small number of Type 3 can be found in this livery with the Exide advert and with 290 embossed on the chassis.

By 1960
smaller upper-deck front windows and
blank destination screen

1960
larger upper-deck front windows

1961/1962
Spun wheels

1962/1963
coloured plastic wheels

Sets of original 'Exide' transfers were available as separate items, proving they could have been added to the sides of the toy either in the factory or at home.
Warning to collectors there are reproduction Exide advertisements about, the style of the lettering is different, as is the quality of the transfer.

A special run was produced for Chloride Batteries Ltd with this covering letter.
The toy had white tyres, and was based on the 1959 casting variant.
This marketing ploy was probably aimed at the younger enthusiasts.

There are four different types of box for 291:
1. a plain version (no image of bus) with Exide Batteries on the flap
2. the normal light yellow box with the extra wording of Exide
3. a darker-yellow box,
4. *no photo* - alternate red and yellow sided box without an image of the bus

Plain boxes were available for the French market and some had a sticker in French on the end flap.

Final stocks of 291 had been cleared from the factory by late 1963.

EXIDE BRAND ADVERTISING - AND YOU

One Bus in every 8 or 9 will carry the Exide message this Winter.

100,000 model buses will fill shop windows and homes with the name Exide this year.

This is name advertising on the grand scale. Use it to increase your battery sales by:

(1) Making sure that, when quoting a customer, you include Exide in the brands you offer.

(2) Displaying an Exide poster or showcard.

(3) Having the four most popular Exide types in stock, on show, charged and ready for use.

Chloride Batteries Limited,
Automotive Division,
Grosvenor Gardens House,
Grosvenor Gardens,
London, S.W.1.

TRA/C.

万人のデラックスコレクション

● 手のひらに乗る ほんものそっくりの自動車

日本で始めて完成された「モデルペット」（TRADE MARK REGISTERED）は外国製品に決しておとらない、精巧度のきわめて高い、実感の溢れた製品です。資材は亜鉛軽合金というきわめて高質な材料が使用されているため、高さ二米のところからコンクリート床に落下させても、割れたり、かけたりしません。モデルペットは各自動車会社の技術的指導と玩具製作の最高スタッフを動員して完成された最高級の製品です。

ヨーロッパ、北米、更に地球をぐるっと一廻りして日本に……ずっしりとした重量感……完璧なフォームの再現……華麗さと豪華なムード……溢れる実感……ミニチュアカーのコレクションで、あなたの生活をお楽しみ下さい。

コレクタークラブへのお誘い

J.M.C.C会員募集

【クラブ入会の手続】
どなたでも自由に入会できます。住所・氏名・年令・職業・所持台数を明記し、年会費三〇〇円を添えてお申込みください。

【会員の特典】
① 月刊誌「コレクター」＝各界のベテランが筆を揃えてミニチュアカーを爽快なタッチで描くマニア必読の解説書＝B6判総アート本文十六頁組、表紙5色刷ビニール引き・1部20円〒8円、年間購読 300円〒共〉無料送付
② 模型展示会及びコンテストのご案内。
③ 所持品コレクションの幹旋。
④ 会員証及びバッジ〈金メッキ製〉、ミニチュアの相互交換。
⑤ ご希望製品の無料送付。
⑥ 情報交換。

申込先
東京都台東区浅草蔵前三の二九二二 旭元玩具製作所内〈電〈八五〉一二二一五〉

英国の名門 CORGI TOYS DINKY TOYS 製品100車種直輸入発売中

Front cover of Japanese Miniatures Collectors Club Catalogue

Special thanks to M Driver for the catalogue.

Type 2 - Cream livery
A puzzle, until fairly recently, has been the all-cream livered variant predominantly with red wheels. Suggestions were that it had been produced for sale in Germany or South Africa.

However recent research indicates it was ordered by Asahi Diecast Models to be sold in Japan, as part of a series for their Japanese Miniatures Collectors Club. For whatever reason it was cancelled but the buses had or were already being made. So the batch was offered for sale in Germany, possibly to a wholesaler based in the Berlin area, where cream double deck buses have operated for many decades.
Hence why so many continue to turn up in the Berlin area.

Type 3, but is this genuine?

Type 2s

Type 3

Catalogue Number 29c & 290

It's often referred to as the AEC Regent III Series 2, which was a real vehicle brought into service in 1947 for the provincial British operator and also for export.

The toy may have been influenced by buses entering service with Liverpool Corporation in the last 1940's. Many considered it to have a "neat and stylish front profile".

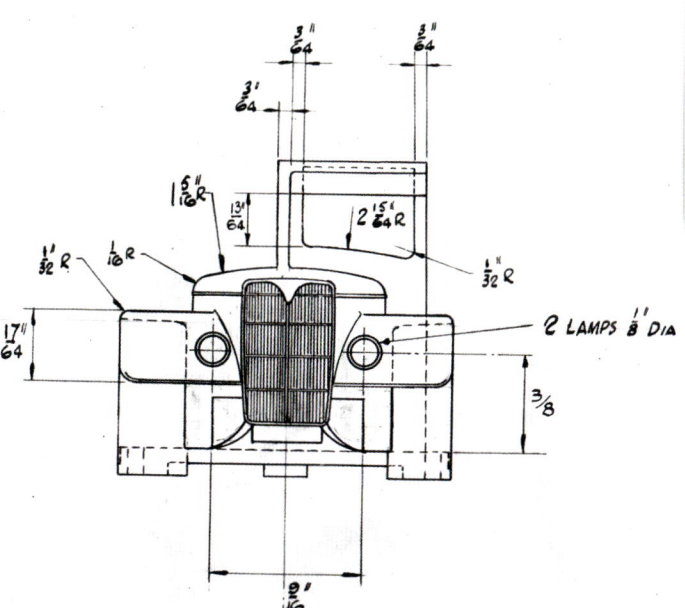

This version of the toy first appeared in 1949 and was re-issued in 1957. The oddity of this variant was that the rear mudguards were cast onto the body, not onto the chassis as previously. The side destination screen is larger than the one on the Type 2 casting.

Also worth noting is that on this version the rear top-deck window was of the enlarged type, while for the more popular Leyland bus this alteration was introduced many years later, in 1961.

With permission from H Clarke

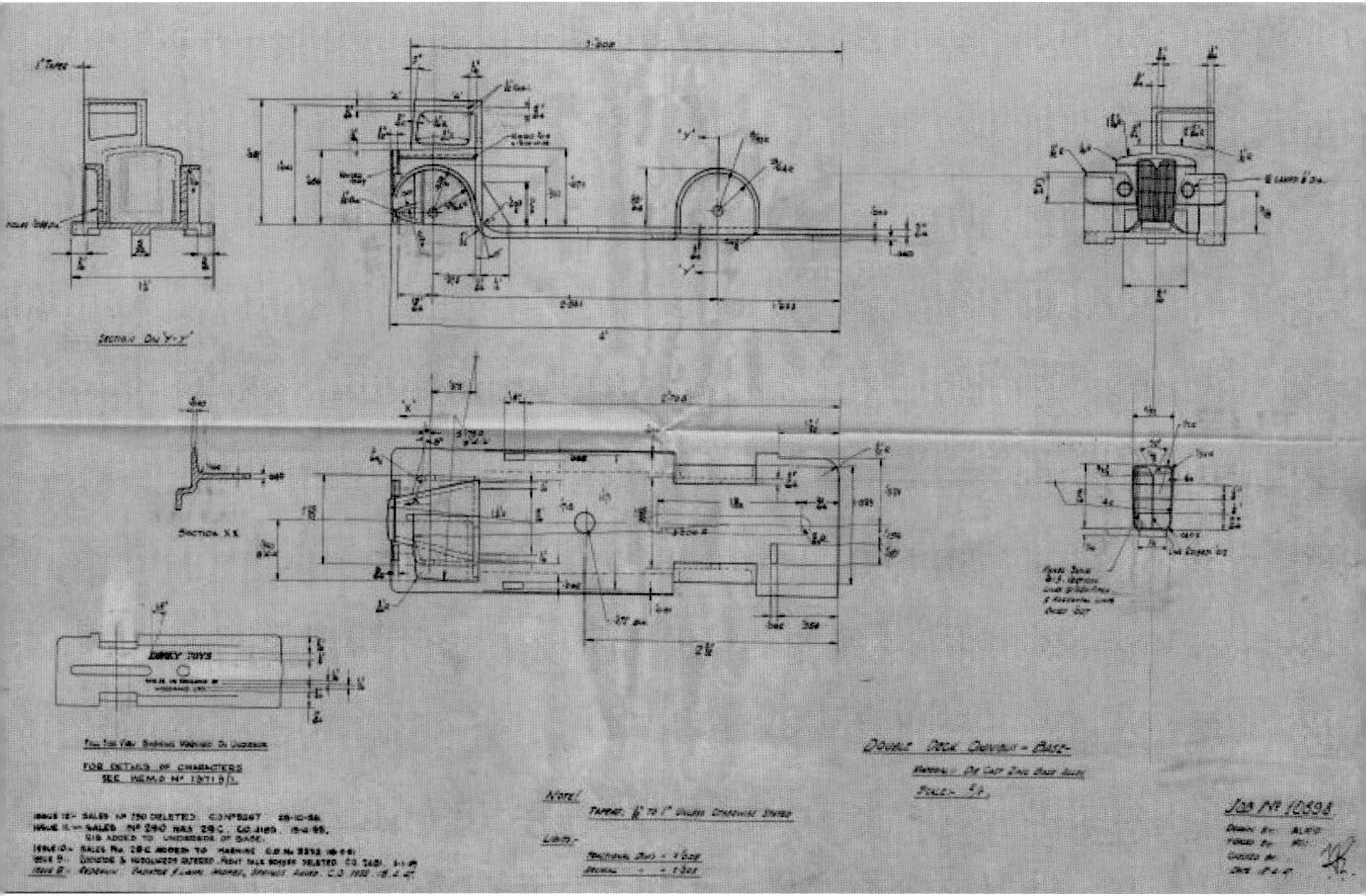

Roof box and no adverts

From my inspections of many Type 3's:
- livery was either red/cream or green/cream, with the wheel hubs always matching the lower body colour
- there are two sizes of the enlarged rear window with the change taking place at an early stage in the production cycle
- in 1952, eight interior ribs were added between the window frames, four on either side
- in 1953, 29c was embossed on the chassis, at the same time as pin-head axles were introduced
- when re-issued in 1957: the roof box had been deleted; 'Dunlop' advertisement was added and the catalogue number was amended to 290
- last examples of this toy were produced in early 1959

There were no special boxes produced for Type 3.
The general assumption is that all the Type 3's were sold in tradeboxes (ie. not boxed individually).

However, it seems likely that some were sold in Type 2 boxes.

Post 1957 as no roof box

35

Quality control at Dinky varied which meant that "oddities" were produced.

Here is a genuine toy with a Leyland body on an AEC chassis. It's been seen in red/cream and green/cream liveries.

It is convincing evidence that there may be interesting variations held by collectors that have never been catalogued.

Type 3 - comparison of all three chassis' - blank / 29c / 290

Type 2 chassis with Type 3 body.
Note the gap behind the rear wheel arches

Photograph was taken in 1957 on the
Meccano production line in
Liverpool.
Copyright owned by
www.20thcenturyimages.co.uk.

Type 1   Type 2   Type 3

Different types of boxes:
1. the original tradebox
2. toy pictured on box with 290/29c printed on the end-flaps, which appeared in 1954
3. light or dark yellow box with 290 printed on its sides which lasted until 1959
4. in 1960 a plain box with alternate red and yellow sides
5. in 1961 a plain box
6. boxed toys were often sent to shops in boxes of 6
7. EXIDE

Boxes with dual numbers are rare because they were printed like this for less than a year.

An interesting 1950s advert used in a transport magazine, showing a variety of Dinky buses.

Corporation Transport - Real or Fake?

For me the most interesting toys to come out of the factory have to be the AEC STL, Leyland Titan, Duple Roadmaster Coach and Routemaster Bus bearing the fleetname of 'Corporation Transport'.

But the question is "Are they fake or real"?

Some people say that they remember buying such toys direct from the factory, which was an option available in those days. However, the 'Corporation Transport' fleetname is only seen on those sold in the early 1960s which is after the Leyland Atlantean had been released.

If they are genuine Dinky toys then the company might have used them as a means of clearing obsolete stock perhaps?

Type 1

There are reproduction fleetnames in circulation which can cause confusion. These can be spotted by comparing them with examples of the original Leyland Atlantean as there are minor differences.

The surface area of the 'Corporation Transport' transfer was increased when the Leyland Atlantean was produced in its green/white livery.

Genuine examples on other toy buses would have been sold before this change, using the original smaller transfers.

Or perhaps Dinky supplied separate 'Corporation Transport' transfers on request as they did for the original 'Exide' advertisement.

There has also been seen an example of an all red 'Exide' bearing a

Type 2

Leyland Atlantean

Correction to Page 40

The two missing words at the bottom are 'Ribble' fleetname.

Correction to Page 40

The two missing words at the bottom are 'Ribble' fleetname.

It's just like the NEW bus on your route

DINKY TOYS
No. 292
LEYLAND ATLANTEAN BUS

This excellent miniature will be the pride of your collection. It is based on that striking new public transport vehicle, the Leyland Atlantean Bus which is a 78-seater. It is 30 ft. in length and 8 ft. wide, with folding entrance and exit door at the front. The Leyland diesel engine, fitted at the rear, develops 125 b.h.p. at 1,800 r.p.m. The model is complete with windows, seating, steering wheel and driver.

Length 4¾ in.   U.K. Price **7/11**

DINKY TOYS
TRADE MARK REGISTERED

MADE BY MECCANO LIMITED

...ssified as PDR1/1, entered fleets from late 1958 and
...t from 1959. They were fitted with Metro-Cammell
...r of low-bridge variants were also delivered to the
...ved its origins to a handful of prototypes produced
...cept of a rear-engined double-deck bus.

...alogue number 292, appeared in July 1962 and
...For once there was a miniature bus based on a
...ent service. Previously Dinky had based their buses
...ossibly, for the first time, there was not only a very
...ould be called a model, especially as it was very
...ilway layouts.

...y with advertisements for 'Regent petrol' and a

41

Published by MECCANO LTD., Binns Road, Liverpool 13, England   Printed by John Waddington Ltd., Leeds & London

Within a few months, a version was offered with the Ribble fleetname which initially didn't have adverts.

The interior plastic seats were either red or cream.

The red seats are normally only found within the castings that have a Ribble fleetname and no adverts.

The chassis fitted into the body via the rear slot with a second slot at the front under the headlights.

Early toys had a complete front entrance/exit door with no lug (casting 1). However later toys had an extra lug (casting 2) for the chassis at the base of the door.

The Ribble and Corporation Transport fleetnames are seen on both castings, and were possibly produced simultaneously for a time.

Casting 1

Casting 2 with lug at bottom of the door

Corporation Transport

A rare example of the chassis from the casting 1, married to the body of casting 2. *They clearly don't fit.*

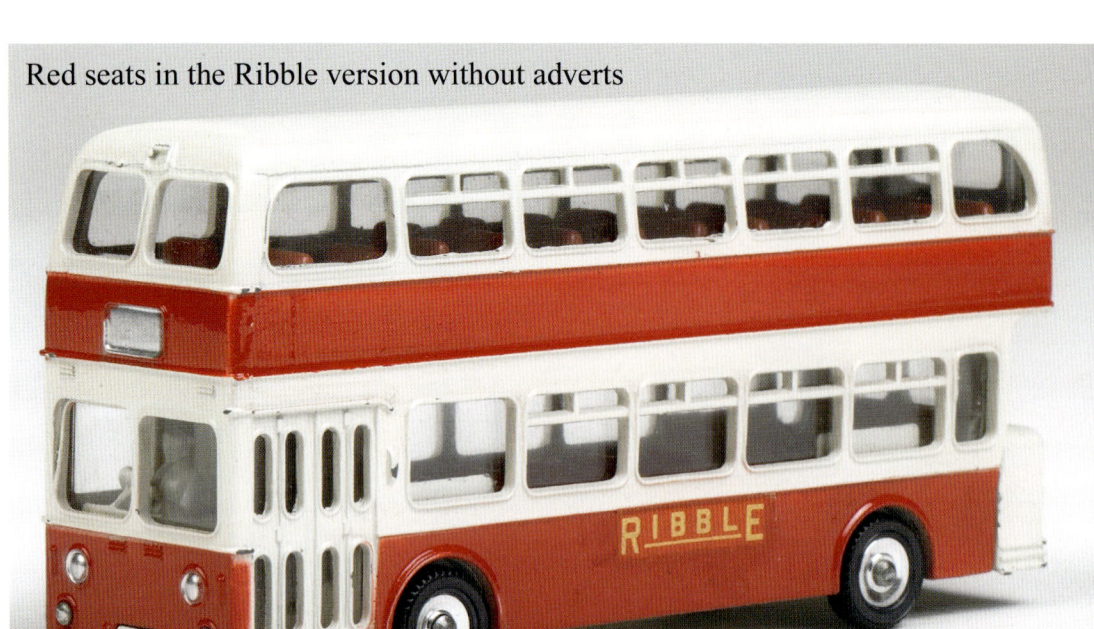

Red seats in the Ribble version without adverts

All are casting 2

Red seats and no adverts so this is a Ribble

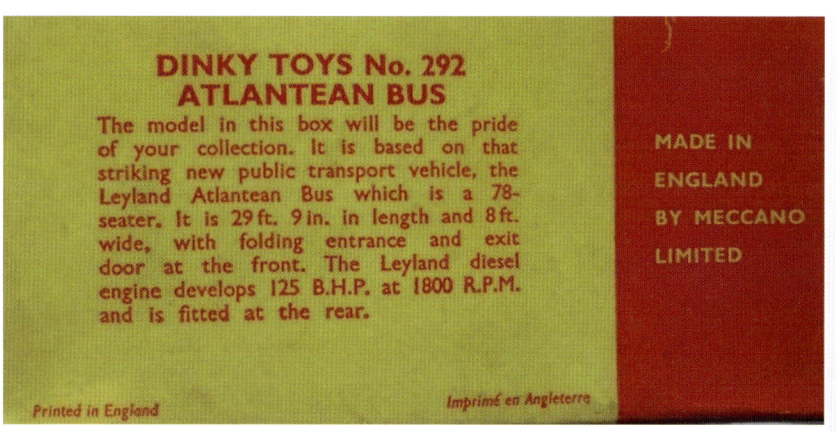

Box designs:

1. Mostly yellow with a one-inch red band around one side listing the special features for which the Dinky toy was famous. There was an image of the actual toy on the front of the box and details of the real vehicle on the back.

   The boxes used for the Ribble variant usually carried a Ribble stamp on the end of the box.

2. Tradebox which held six boxed toys and carried catalogue number 292 on its sides.

Box end displaying the **Ribble stamp**

"The Old meets the New"
As the old toy nears the end of its life, the new one gets ready to take over.

Perhaps a prototype for the upcoming Atlantean City Bus or did someone create it? Does anyone know?

DINKY TOYS

449 Chevrolet El Camino Pick-up Truck. 4⅜" – 111 mm.

436 Atlas Copco Compressor Lorry. 3½" – 89 mm.

292 Atlantean Bus 4¾" – 121 m

290 Double Deck Bus. DUNLOP. 4" – 102 mm.

291 London Bus EXIDE.

An original 1956 catalogue for the very first Leyland Atlantean as would have been given away to promote the real bus.
Plus the Dinky bus in the same livery.

RUSH HOUR isn't CRUSH HOUR anymore

Beating the peak rushes is always a problem. At least it was—until the Leyland Atlantean arrived. Now, over 40 municipalities and bus operating companies have proved this 72/78 seater to be the answer.

Greater-than-ever seating capacity; driver-controlled, low-step, front-entrance; quick acceleration from the Leyland 125 h.p. diesel; exceptional manoeuvrability in traffic all combine to make the Atlantean first choice on more and more city and inter-urban routes.

And there are many other advantages. Fleets can meet higher traffic demands without corresponding vehicle and mileage increases. Greater loads reduce extent to which fares must be raised to meet higher operational costs. Accidents-per-mile ratio are far lower than with a rear-entrance double-decker without doors. And, relieved of platform duties, conductors have far more time for fare collection at peak hour rushes.

With all that, the Atlantean costs little more than a normal double-decker, is at least as cheap to run, yet has far greater profit potential. Follow the trend—switch now to Atlanteans.

Wide, driver-controlled doors with low-step front-entrance, speed loading and unloading and provide added safety.

Simplified controls give smooth, effortless driving under all conditions.

Leyland ATLANTEAN

LEYLAND MOTORS LTD·Leyland·Lancs.
Sales Division: Berkeley Square House,
Berkeley Square, London, W.1.
Tel: GROsvenor 6050

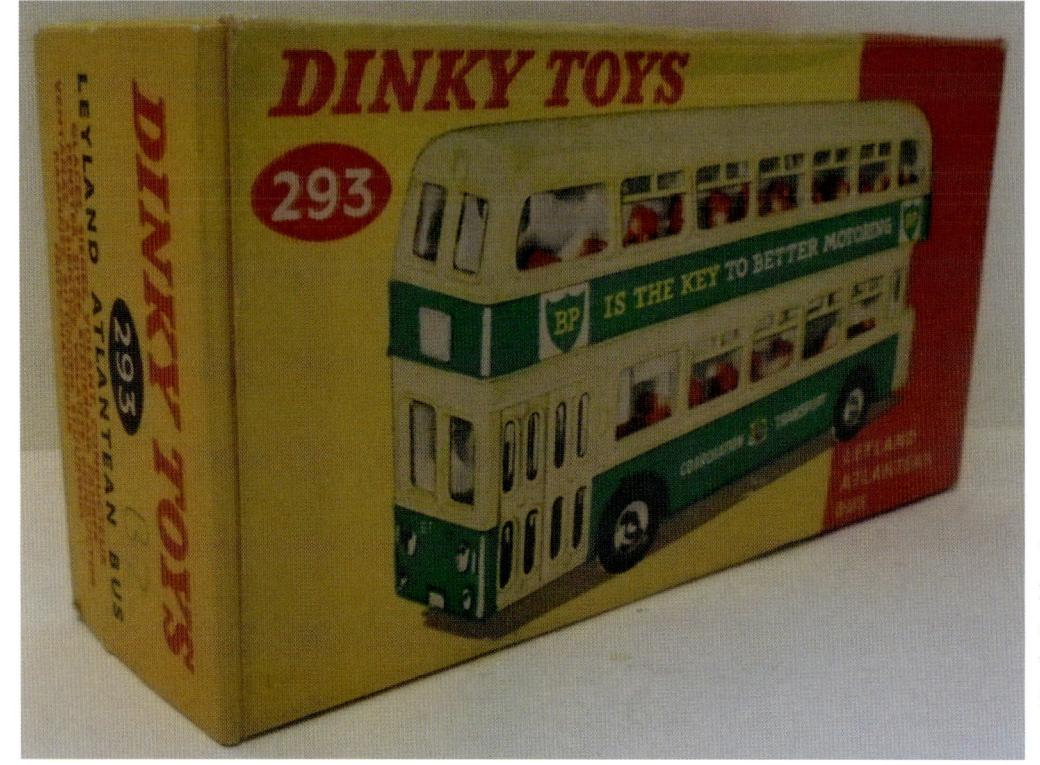

The second livery appeared in 1963, with a catalogue number of 293: green/white and carried advertisements for BP petrol. This livery was only applied to the second casting, (ie. extra lug under the front door).

Again interior seats were either red or cream. Although red was the dominant colour.

In 1964 there was a minor change to the fleetname transfer as it now covered a larger surface after the coat of arms.

Red seats

Cream seats

The image on the individual box featured the green/white liveried bus with red seats. The image was much larger than on previous boxes and appeared on the front and back giving it a more 'modern look'. The toy description was demoted to one of the end flaps, whilst the red side band described the item contained in the box.

In 1964 there was a third casting which saw the addition of six ribs to the roof of the model.
Was this to assist the casting or to make the model look more realistic?

This version is not as common as the 1963 variant. The number produced was probably equal to those in red/cream with Ribble fleetnames.

Routemaster London Bus

The AEC Routemaster (RM) double-decker bus was designed by London Transport and built by the Associated Equipment Company (AEC) and Park Royal Vehicles (PRV). The first prototype appeared in 1954, causing gasps of astonishment from passengers in the London area as it dwarfed the double-deck buses and trolley buses they were used to.

The RM class was in service from 1959 to 1968, replacing the trolleybuses which were all withdrawn by 1962.

An article on this bus appeared in the 1964 June issue of the Meccano Magazine, with a full-colour advertisement for the toy on the back cover. It confirmed that Meccano had approached London Transport (LT) with a view to producing a new toy bus based on those serving the

'Tern Shirts' was the first adverts

capital. They asked LT for advice on the model to choose and the details they should incorporate for their miniature version.

The choice was the AEC Routemaster double-decker bus and it was given catalogue number 289.

The casting was a good representation of the real bus and caught the proportions of this now classic design.

Jim Bailey, Roger's dad, was a bus driver in the 1950s and 1960s

50

6   BUS & COACH   DECEMBER 1959

ALUMINIUM MAKES BIGGER BUSES LIGHTER

The Routemaster is the largest two-axle bus ever to go into service with London Transport. Chassisless construction gives lightness with strength and these 64-seater buses are actually lighter than the smaller ones they replace. Aluminium panelling and special extrusions are supplied by British Aluminium to Park Royal Vehicles Ltd who are building 850 Routemasters.

The BRITISH ALUMINIUM Co Ltd

NORFOLK HOUSE   ST JAMES'S SQUARE   LONDON SW1

AP378

THIS MONTH'S NEW DINKY MODELS

London Transport's ROUTEMASTER

Run your own bus services with this famous London Transport double decker ● Just like the real thing ● Seats for 64 passengers ● Staircase ● Driver and clippie ● Real advertisements ● Bright red bodywork.

MODEL 289. LENGTH 4¼"   **8/11**

Exact in every detail Clippie is reaching for bell. Carries money bag and ticket machine. She and the driver both dressed in London Transport uniform.

AND THE CAR WITH A FLAIR—THE FORD CONSUL CORSAIR

Opening Bonnet
Up-and-down windows
Jewelled headlights

Own this exciting new car from Ford with its many real-life Dinky features ● Bonnet opens to reveal engine ● Jewelled headlights reflect light ● Sliding windows ● Steering wheel ● Prestomatic finger-tip steering ● Finished in yellow metallic, red seats.

MODEL 130. 4¼" LONG.   **5/11**

Always something new from

DINKY TOYS
precision-engineered by Meccano Limited

Published by Thomas Skinner & Co. (Publishers) Ltd., St. Alphage House, Fore St., London, E.C.2. Printed by James Cond Ltd., Charlotte St., Birmingham 3

Maurine Bailey, Roger's mum, was a conductress for Coventry Corporation Transport from 1956 to 1971 before becoming a driver then inspector.

The interior included plastic windows, stairs, and until 1978 a driver in the cab and a conductress on the rear platform. It came with adverts and destination screens, in this case for route 221. It was such a good miniature that it was difficult to know whether to call it a toy or a model.

Advertisements for 'Tern Shirts' were used for the initial production. Being replaced in 1965 by an advertisement for 'Schweppes' which lasted until 1969. The colour of the seating for these toys were white/ cream. The advert was then replaced by 'Esso Safety Grip Tyres (Esso)' and lasted for 10 years, until the end of production. .

Spun wheels were used initially followed by cast wheels to be finally replaced by plastic speedwheels.

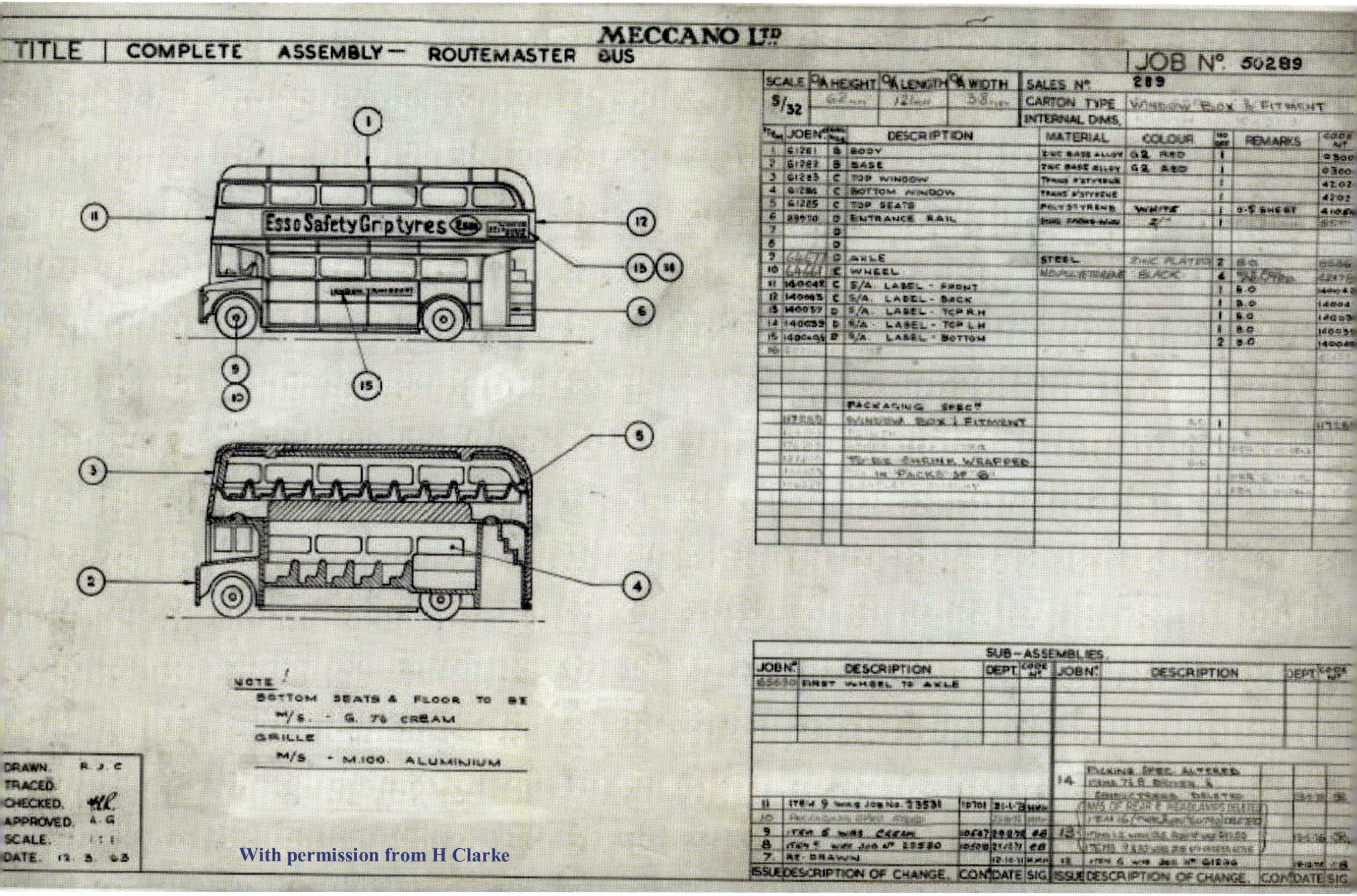

With permission from H Clarke

From 1973 modifications were made to the window bars until they were all eventually removed. However there must have been several versions of the mould being changed in different ways with respect to this removal because of the mix of variants to be found. By 1976/1977, all window bars had been removed. *So there are plenty of variations to look out for.*

Photos here shows 4 variations of the post-1970 toy (ie 'Esso' adverts) in order of age:
1. Spun wheels, painted headlights, cream upper and lower-deck seats, front window bars and some side bars
2. Cast wheels, painted headlights, mid-blue upper and lower-deck seats, only one front window has a bar and several side window bars
3. From 1976: plastic speedwheels, no painted headlights, no painted rear lights, light-blue upper-deck seats, mid-blue lower-deck seats, window bars only at front.
4. From 1978: plastic speedwheels, cream upper-deck seats, red lower-deck seats, no driver, no conductress, no window bars. Toy in photo was produced in 1979 because no adverts at the front and unpainted speedwheels..

54

These photos are showing a toy that was produced from 1978.
Note:
- Plastic speedwheels
- Headlights not painted
- Rear lights not painted
- Red lower-deck seating
- No bars at any of the windows
- No driver
- No conductress

This toy is not yet the final version produced because it does still have adverts at the front and silver painted speedwheels.

1968 saw the first 'promotional' run - a standard issue bus with black-on-gold advertisement for the 'Festival of London Stores', applied to both sides.

In the 1970's there was a famous special for Madame Tussaud's which was displayed in a hanging box or card tray box. Predominantly the livery was red, but the advertisements have also been seen on a silver model. Four different casting :
1. All window bars, advert blue lettering on a white background
2. Missing upper-window bars: rear on nearside, front on offside; advert blue lettering on a white background
3. All window bars, light blue seats, advert white lettering on a blue background
4. Front window bars only, mid blue lower-deck seats, plastic speedwheels, headlights not painted, advert white lettering on a blue background

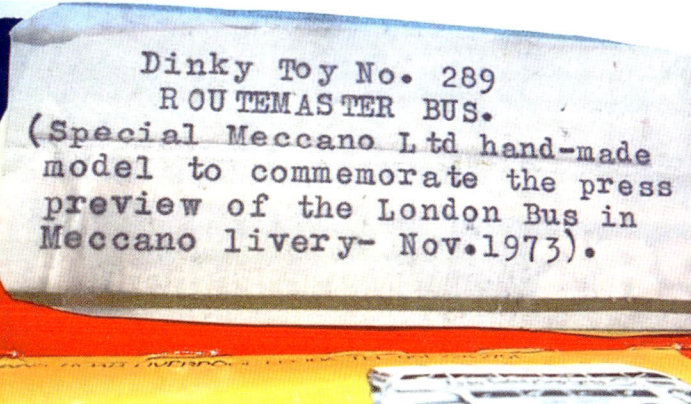

A small number were produced in gold, for a press launch in 1973.

Another interesting version in gold is a Belgium promotional for 'thollembeek & fils'.

57

Towards the end of production, a special run was made for a shop in Blackpool. It had the famous cream livery of the real buses that ply their trade along the Blackpool Golden Mile. The toy was presented in a hanging box with advertisements for self-application, of 'Visit Blackpool Zoo', 'Blackpool Illuminations' and the fleet name 'Blackpool Transport'.

Some 'promotionals' had their advertisements applied in the factory. Whereas others were done once they had left, *which could explain why some toys have no adverts*.

Various advertisements have appeared:
- 'K Shoes of England K Shoes', using red and blue lettering appeared from the late 1960's presented in an impressive display stand with a background image of the Houses of Parliament, *possibly for use in shops*
- 'Fordath' in an all-red livery which was normally presented for display in a plain white box
- 'Esso Safety Grip Tyres Esso' and 'Ever-Ready Batteries for Life' on all-silver or all-gold toys, displayed in a hanging box
- 'Dinkyprint' in a red livery, with red lettering on white background together with one of their wallpaper labels on the display box. It was produced in the late 1970's for a wallpaper manufacturer to promote their range of wallpaper designs
- 'Shoplinker' appears on toys in red and yellow livery

There are others, but one problem is that many were produced close to the end of production, therefore it does prove difficult to verify those that have been factory-produced.

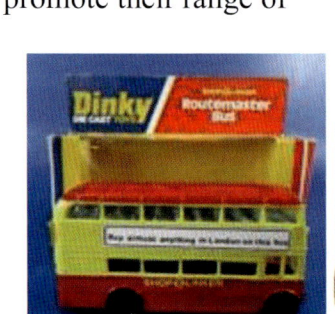

It was also issued as a kit under catalogue number 1017.

There were two different types of packaging: one was in the more common wrap-over style and the other was on a simple card.

A variety of display and presentation boxes were produced:

1. Initially they were the fully enclosed type with artwork showing the 'Tern Shirts' advertisements, then 'Schweppes' and finally 'Esso'
2. Later years of production saw the hanging box used and for presentation sets
3. Finally came the card-tray which was also used for the bus and London 'black cab' gift set towards the end of production
4. There was also the rarer gold transparency box
5. Once the factory had closed, the surplus buses were sold in a rather cheap-looking enclosed yellow box, of which few examples survive

Atlantean City Bus

This vehicle is often referred to as a Leyland Atlantean, but it was actually based on a Daimler Fleetline initially intended for central Manchester duties. *It clearly has a Daimler bustle, so it's strange that they've always been referred to as being based on the Leyland.*

Originally produced for the South East Lancashire and North East Cheshire Passenger Transport Executive, ("SELNEC") formed in 1969 and sub-divided into three divisions: Central, Northern and Southern. The business became known as Greater Manchester Transport in 1974.

The first prototypes arrived in 1970-1971. They were numbered EX1-6, and later 5466-5471, but the ideas in their design are to be found in the original Mancunians built for Manchester Corporation. The first was delivered in 1968 and the chassis being a mix of Daimler and Leyland.

Manchester and Coventry were the first operators to put into service double-deck buses designed for one-man operation.

Forty-eight were made for SELNEC with fleet numbers 7206-51, plus 7280/1 initially ordered for Bury Corporation, plus EX17-21(later 6250-6254). The Northern Counties' body was 9.5 metres long, with a central exit and seating for 72 passengers with standing room for an additional 20. The balance of the order was made up of vehicles with a single entrance/exit door. All deliveries from 1973 onwards were of the single-door variety.

The toy originally appeared in 1973 and it has been suggested that it's based on one of the vehicles listed above. Evidence now suggests that when Meccano visited the factory, buses 7280/81 were actually present.

289 Routemaster London Bus 121 mm

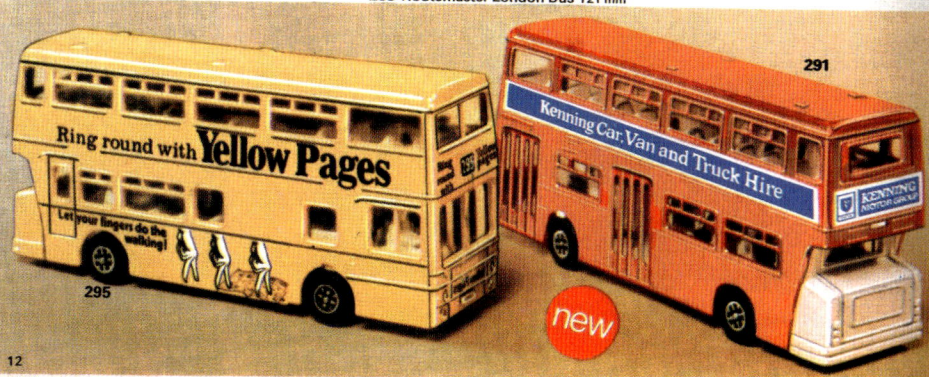

295 Atlantean Bus 123 mm

291 Atlantean City Bus 123 mm

With permission from H Clarke

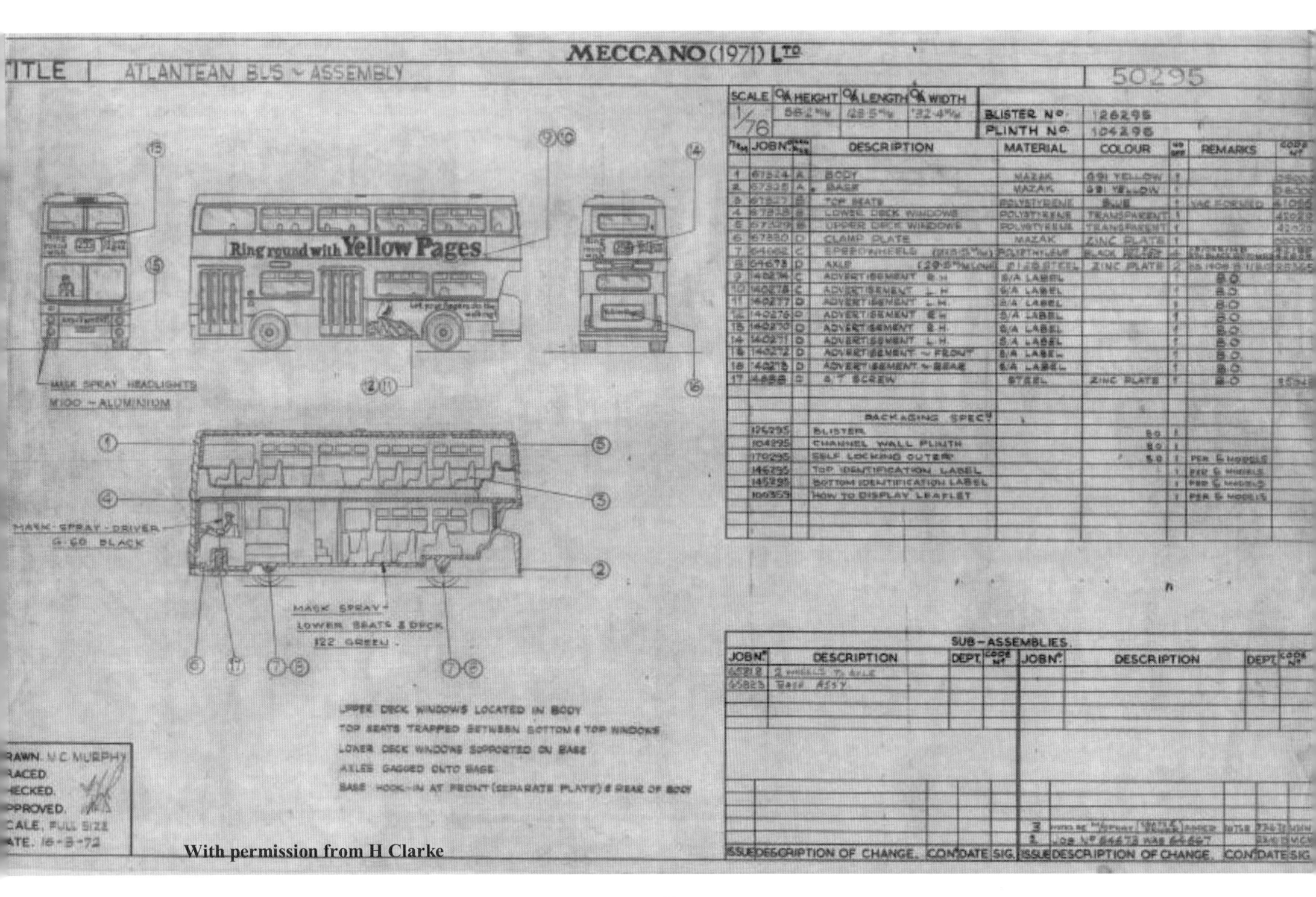

In 1973, the 'Yellow Pages' Atlantean Bus, with catalogue number 295, was produced and lasted for three years. It was based on a real vehicle with all-over advertising, that was certainly in service in 1974.

Livery: two shades of yellow (light and much darker) plus silver. The chassis was usually the same shade as the body.

The seats on the upper and lower decks were normally blue of varying shades. The darker yellow toy has been seen with blue upper-deck seats and yellow lower-deck seats. A few of the lighter yellows were produced with a white chassis and white seats.

In 1974 the Atlantean City Bus, with catalogue number 291, was to be the second variant. Production lasted until 1978. The livery was a deep orange, though the shade does vary. The chassis was initially white, although later a blue variant was produced. Seats were usually painted to match the chassis colour, but a few have been found with a combination of white chassis and blue seats.

The boxes for this series of Dinky bus:

1. The card tray with a clear lid was initially used, especially for all the 'Yellow Pages' variants and also for some of the later orange examples.
2. Replaced by the hanging box. Orange version was sold in both types of box. Also the Silver Jubilee Bus was sold in this type of box.
3. Tradebox which held 6 of the card tray boxes

With permission from H Clarke

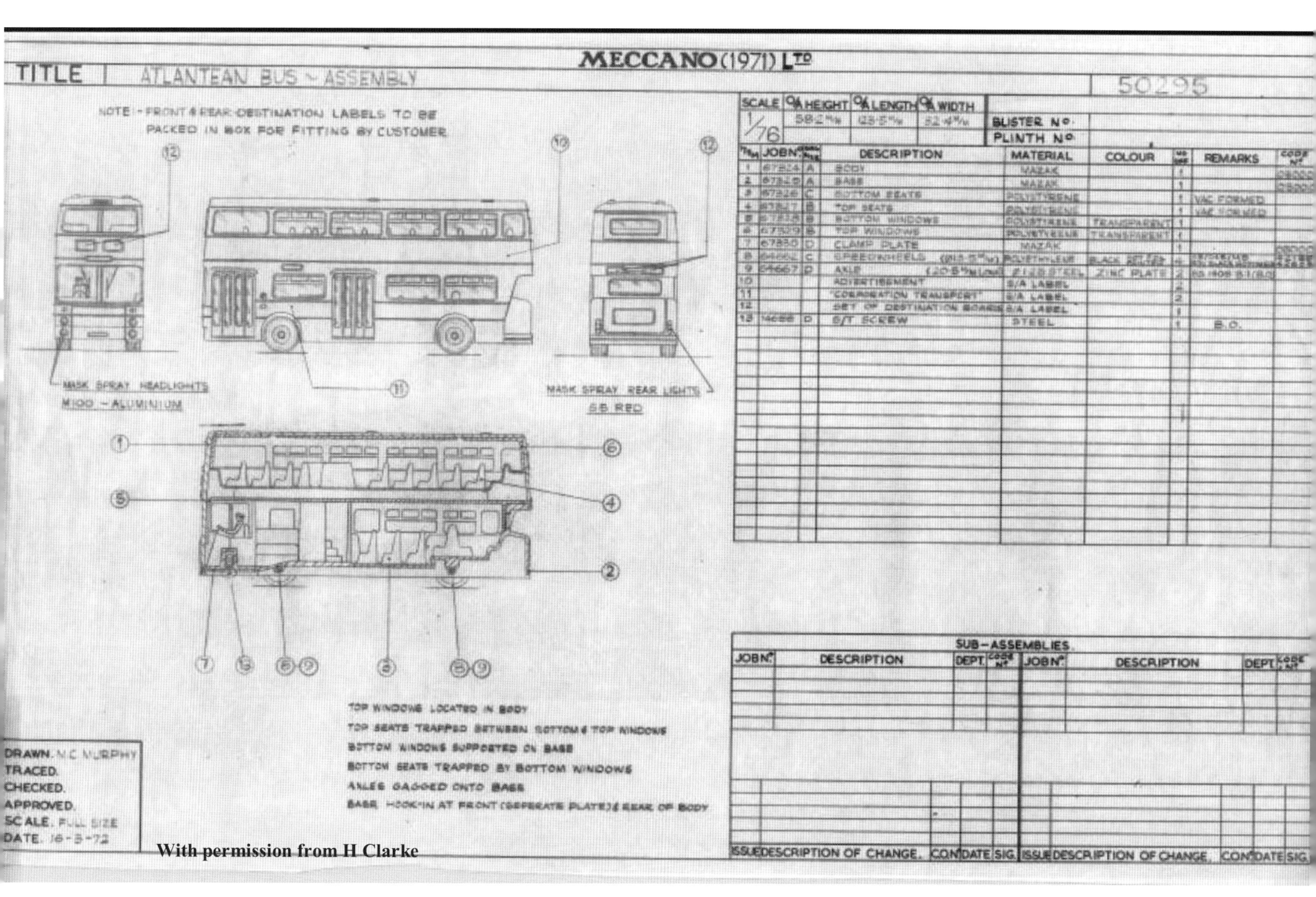

1977 was an interesting year for miniature bus enthusiasts because many toy and model manufacturers produced buses in silver to commemorate the Silver Jubilee of Queen Elizabeth II. Dinky's catalogue number for the Jubilee version was 297, of which there were several types:

- The general release toy advertised the 'Silver Jubilee' and had a fleet name of 'National'
- Another version advertised 'Woolworths' with a fleet name of 'The Queen's Silver Jubilee 1977'
- A special version carrying an advertisement for the 'Model Bus Federation' as its way of celebrating the Jubilee. Possibly only 100 were made at a price of £2.30. The advertisements were applied after leaving the factory.

All versions had light-blue coloured seats, the first use of this colour interior.

They appeared in a special hanging box that was only available for the period surrounding the Jubilee celebrations.

A small batch of red liveried vehicles was produced bearing either 'Esso' or 'Kennings' advertisements and fleet names for London Transport.

Also seen in silver, were toys with 'Esso' adverts on the sides - stickers normally seen on the Routemaster.
Nothing is known of the origins of these versions. Perhaps you know more?

A small number were produced in gold to commemorate the press preview of the London Bus in Meccano - Nov 1973, as were some Routemasters.

A promotional model was made in white for 'London & Manchester Assurance'.

67

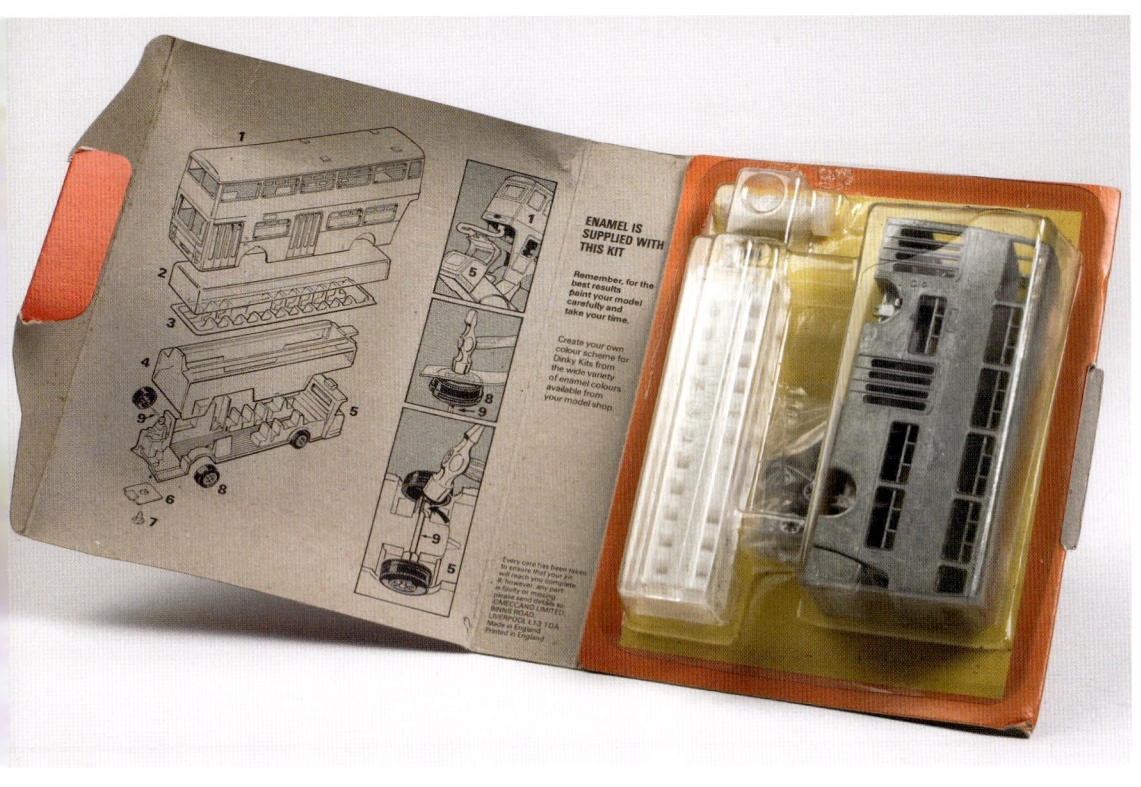

A special deal was struck between Meccano and the Model Bus Federation giving their members the opportunity to purchase some unpainted Atlantean castings directly from the manufacturers. The announcement came in the August 1973 issue of their Journal, with a price tag of 70p, including postage!

This coincided with the announcement of the release of the model, and so was hot news to the members and warranted the few days delay of the publication of the August issue to carry the news. 4,500 of these were sold to members of the MBF, which included some of the later kits.

From 1974 to 1976, a kit version with catalogue number 1018, was produced and proved popular. The kit came in a box with exploded assembly instructions and a small amount of white paint and transfers for 'National'. Upper-deck seats were usually cream/white, but some exist with blue seats.

Prices of official kit as advertised in the MBF's Journal:
- April 1974 Issue - 65p each (60p each if ordering 10 or more)
- May 1974 Issue - 75p each (70p each if ordering 10 or more)
- June 1974 Issue - 80p each (75p each if ordering 10 or more)
- By the middle of 1975 £1.05 for a single kit.

As a price comparison, the first official release of the model in 1973 in 'Yellow Pages' livery was 89p.

The dealer John Gay commissioned a special run of 500 blue and 500 white Atlanteans. The body and chassis were in the same colour. Lower-deck seats were the body colour and upper-deck seats were the same light blue as had been used in the Silver Jubilee versions. The advertisements on these toys were the standard 'Kennings' which were much in evidence at that time.

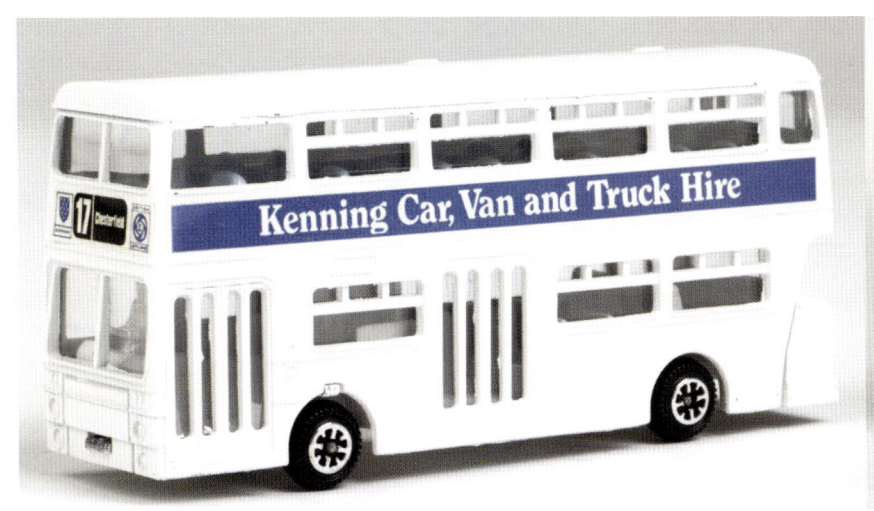

Streamlined Bus

A Holland Coachcraft Van was at the Commercial Motor Show in 1933 and probably represented the ultimate in streamlined styling, built on Commer or Morris Commercial chassis, but few were ever produced.

It was the Holland Coachcraft Van that Meccano based their toy on and gave it a catalogue number of 31. It was produced between 1935 and 1936 without much success. The mould was altered to create the bus variant for production from 1936, having a catalogue number of 29b. The original window pillars were found to be too thin, so the mould was soon modified giving thicker pillars. *No real buses were ever made by Holland Coachcraft only vans*.

It's been suggested that 29b was influenced by an *ultra modern* streamlined bus put into service by Liverpool Corporation in 1935, which ran between the Adelphi Hotel, Lime Street Station and Speke Aerodrome. This bus had a Dennis Ace chassis and was designed to look natural and distinguishable from the run-of-the-mill coaches. Due to the Second World War the vehicle was later converted into a van after the cessation of civilian air passenger services.

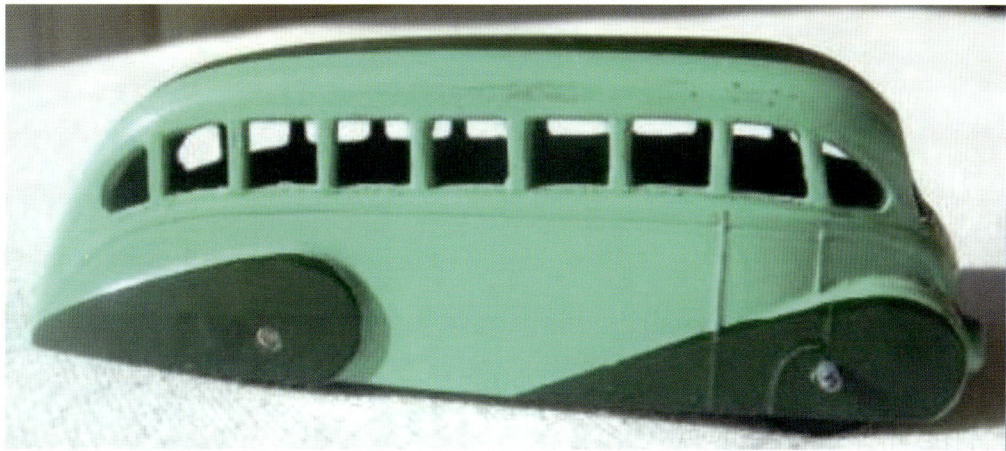

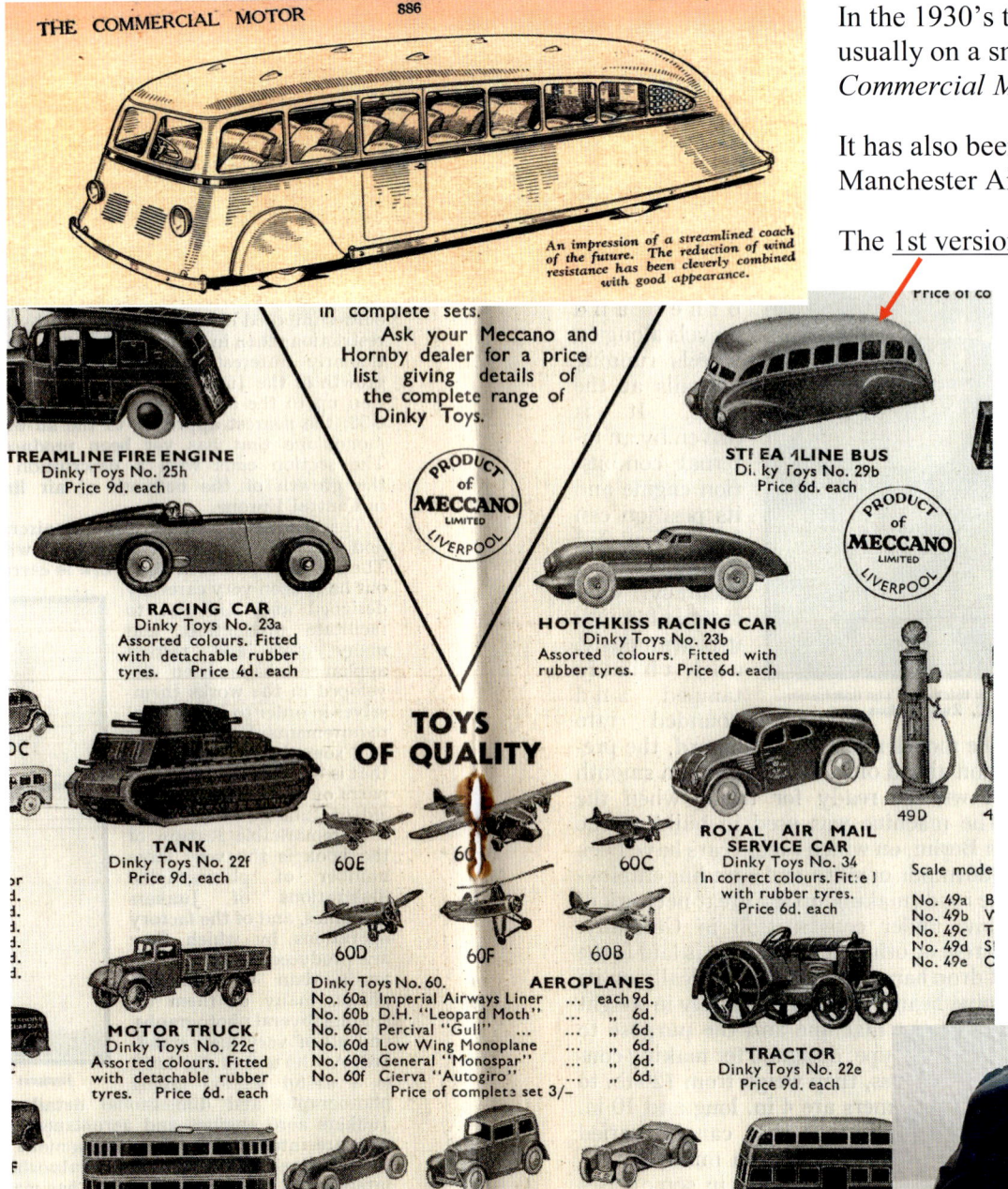

In the 1930's the idea of streamlining buses and vehicles was becoming popular. They were usually on a small chassis, *as can be seen in the sketch on the left that appeared in the Commercial Motor magazine.*

It has also been suggested that 29b was possibly influenced by a vehicle that served Manchester Airport from 1935 to 1939, a unique Crossley Delta with a 20 seater body.

The 1st version of the toy, was in colours: green (light and dark), orange, red, maroon, yellow, blue (light and dark). They all had cream above their lower window line and down tail. There was a rear window with two parallel grooves running from its bottom corners to the base of the rear panel.

The 2nd version was in production until sometime in 1940. It used the same mould but with a different livery. There was an all over colour with a second colour which extended upwards from above the front window tapering the whole length of the roof to the rear window and continuing to taper down between the two grooves to a centre point at the base of the rear panel. The wheel spats were also painted with the second colour.

The colour combinations were:

cream/dark blue, green/dark green, yellow/orange, red/maroon, turquoise/red, light grey/red, light green/green, blue /red, blue/dark blue, dark blue/light blue.

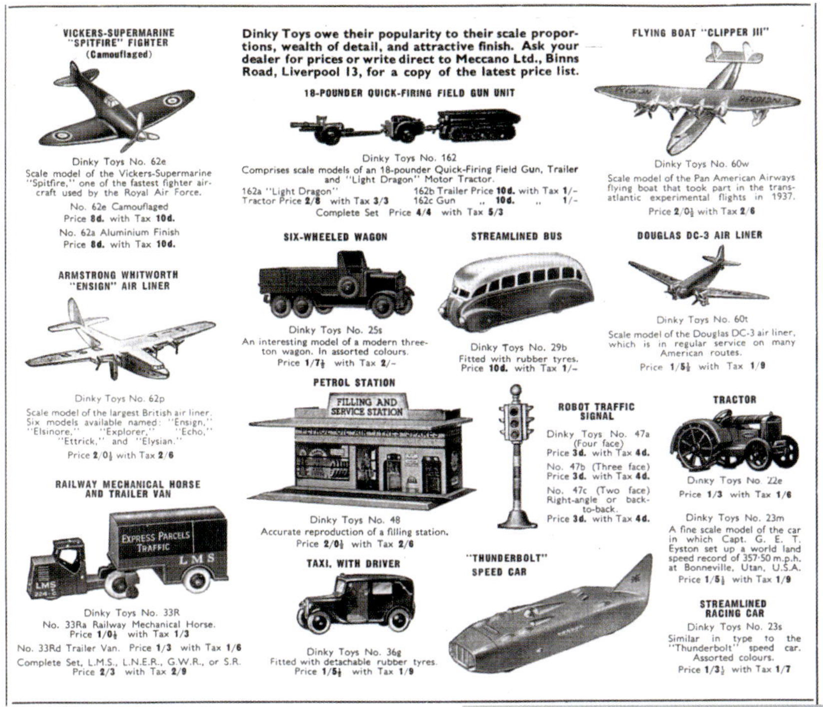

The 3rd version produced just after the war, late 1945 or early 1946, had a slight variation in livery. This time the second paint colour tapered over the roof to the rear window but then extended down from the window corners fully covering the rear panel between the two grooves to the bottom. Again the wheel spats were painted with the second colour.

The colour combinations were:

      green/dark green, light green/mid green, blue/dark blue, light grey/red, cream/blue.

The 4th version again had a variation in livery with only the wheel spats being painted with the second colour. Few of this version would had been produced, as it was not long before the final version hit the toyshops.

The 5th version had a different casting with the back being fully enclosed (ie. no rear window). This modification had taken place by 1948. The livery was like its predecessor (ie. only the wheel spats were painted in the second colour).

The colour combinations were: light grey/red, light grey/blue, green/dark green, dark green/mid green, pale blue/mid blue, mid blue/dark blue.

All versions of the Streamline Buses were only ever sold in a tradebox of six.

However the bus did appear in 1947 as part of Gift Set number 6 Commercial Vehicles, lasting about two years.

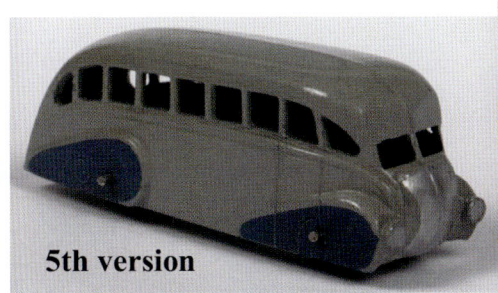

1st version

5th version

Photograph by D. Wallace

Examples of 5th versions

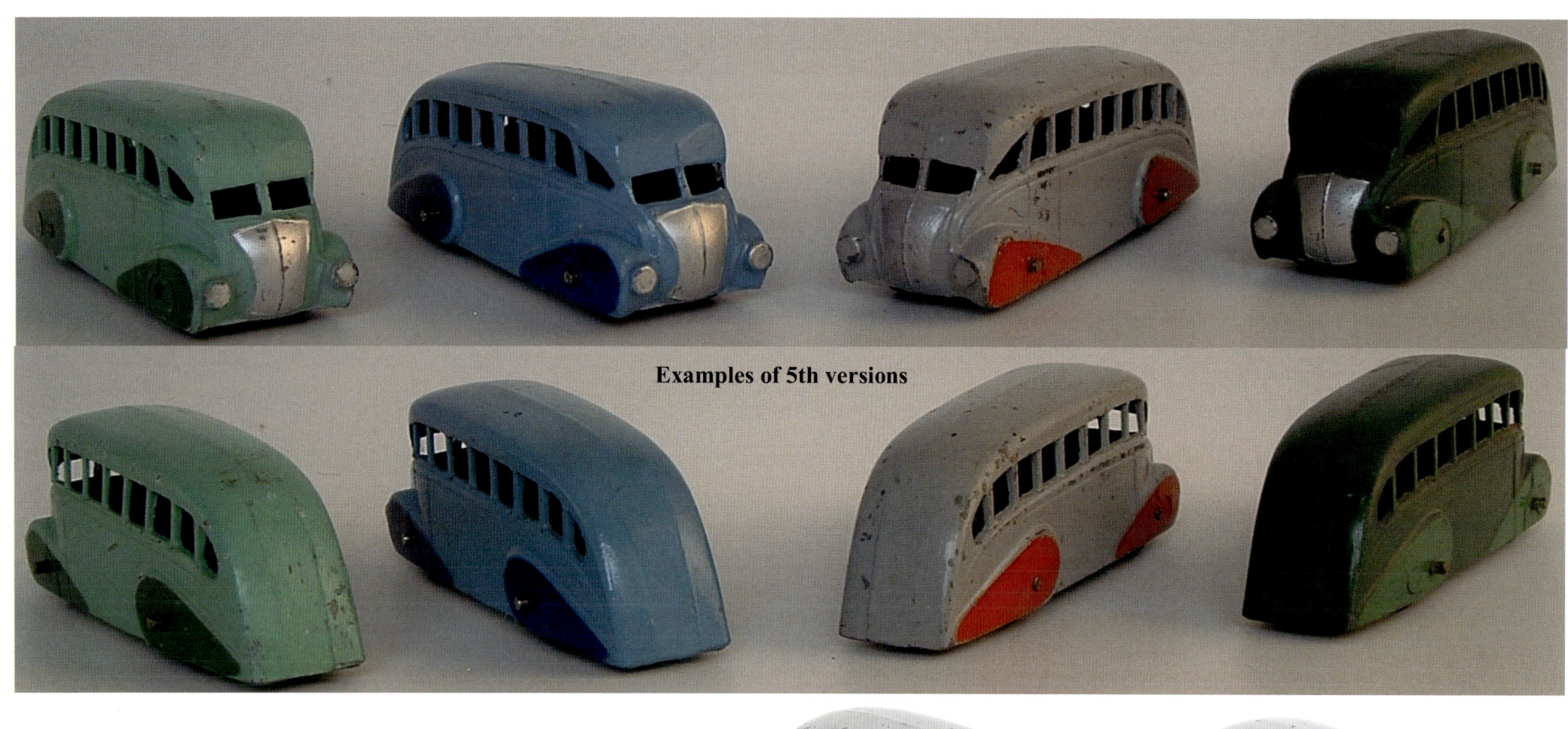

4th or 5th version

3rd version

4th or 5th versions

72

Four of the five stages in this toy's evolution (versions 2 to 5). Left to Right:
- pre-war with the tapered stripe,
- early post-war with the full stripe,
- later post-war with no stripe
- final version with no rear window.

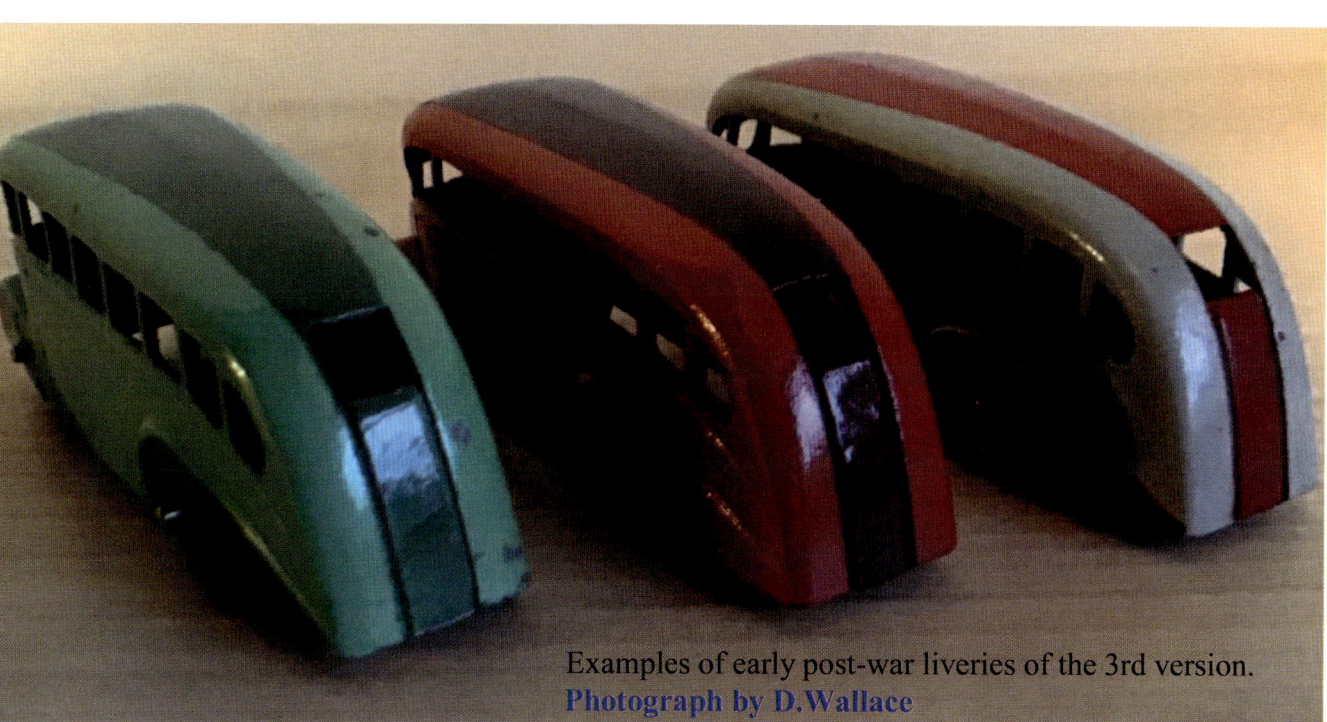

Examples of early post-war liveries of the 3rd version.
Photograph by D.Wallace

73

Single Deck Bus

From 1947 to about 1950, the half-cab single deck bus and coach ruled the roads for new orders, but by 1951 they were largely considered obsolete and very few orders were being placed.

Many collectors believe the Dinky toy is based on a Guy chassis.

The body of the toy is often said to be Duple in style, but this is difficult to prove. The curved waistlines of the toy are clearly in the contemporary coach idiom of the period that were used by many manufacturers around the country, such as Saunders, Yeates, Beadle, Park Royal, Windover, Heaver, Roe and of course Duple. Interestingly manufacturer Santus of Wigan produced a body very similar in style to the Dinky toy. This firm prospered after WWll.

The toy was released in March 1948 under catalogue number 29e but only lasted four years in production, probably reflecting the relatively short life of the original on which it was modelled.

It was only ever available in a tradebox, not lasting long enough to be issued in individual boxes.

Santus of Wigan

Photograph taken in 1950 on the Meccano production line in Liverpool.

Copyright owned by www.20thcenturyimages.co.uk.

3rd versions

1st version

There is no known casting variation except for a slightly different style of rivet being used as production progressed.

Three different liveries were available: cream with blue stripe; blue with darker blue stripe; green with a darker green stripe.

All three were originally produced with black wheel hubs and a single colour line along the bottom of the body.

The second version saw the wheel hub colour matching the main body colour whilst still retaining the additional body line along the bottom.

The third version saw the deletion of the body line.

The green variant can be found with light or dark green wheel hubs.

The shades of green vary, but often this can only be seen when two models are placed together. (To a lesser extent, this is also true of the blue version.)

1st version

2nd version

1st version

3rd version

Photograph taken in 1950 on the Meccano production line in Liverpool.

Copyright owned by www.20thcenturyimages.co.uk.

Luxury Coach

The Maudslay Marathon Mark II, introduced in 1947, and the later Mark III, were very successful vehicles, with 600 sales of the latter between 1948 and 1950. The absorption of Maudslay (along with Crossley) by AEC in 1948 was a form of natural selection because many AEC components were already being supplied to Maudslay.

This style appeared in 1947 alongside the more traditional style of a half-cab single deck coach which was quickly losing its appeal. It was a very popular design that found favour with many of the independent operators around the country. The original vehicle made an appearance at the 1948 Commercial Motor Show.

The Luxury Coach toy was based on the Maudslay Marathon Mark III with what is normally considered to be a Duple body with 33 coach seats.

The toy was in production from April 1951 until 1959.

It was originally given catalogue number 29G but was later renumbered to 281.

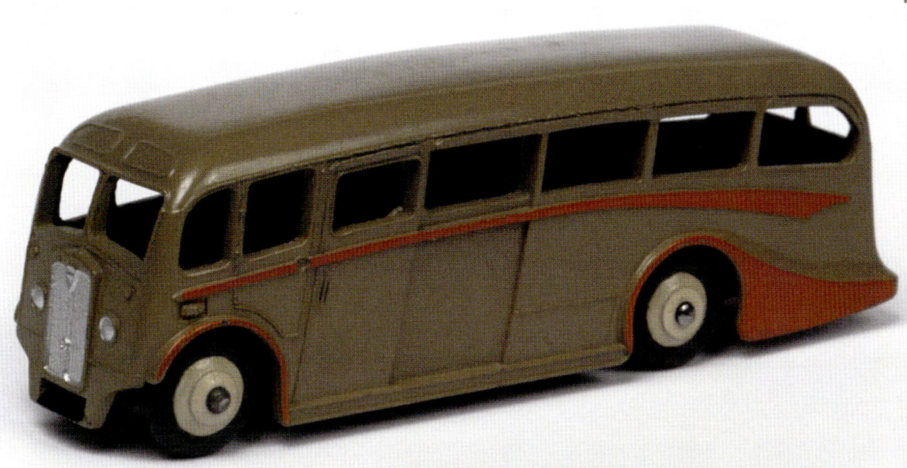

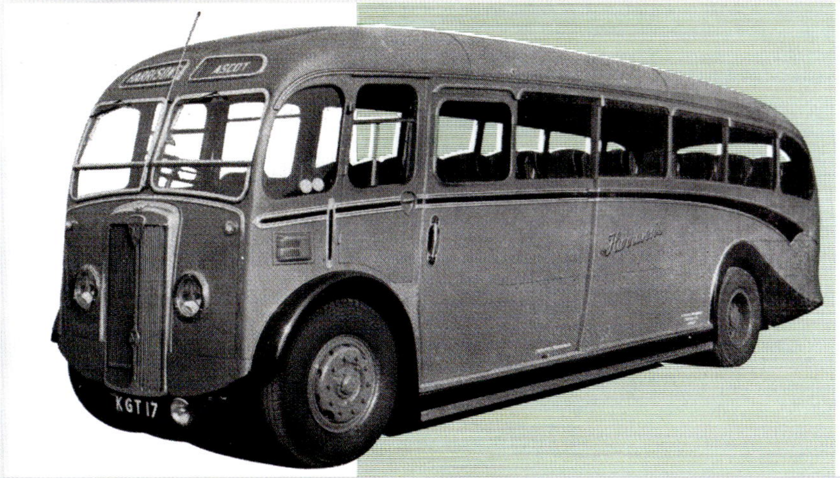

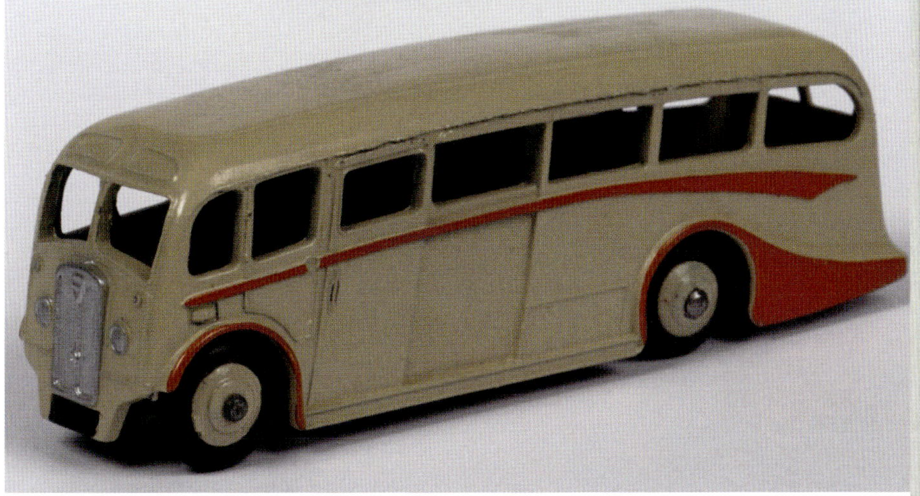

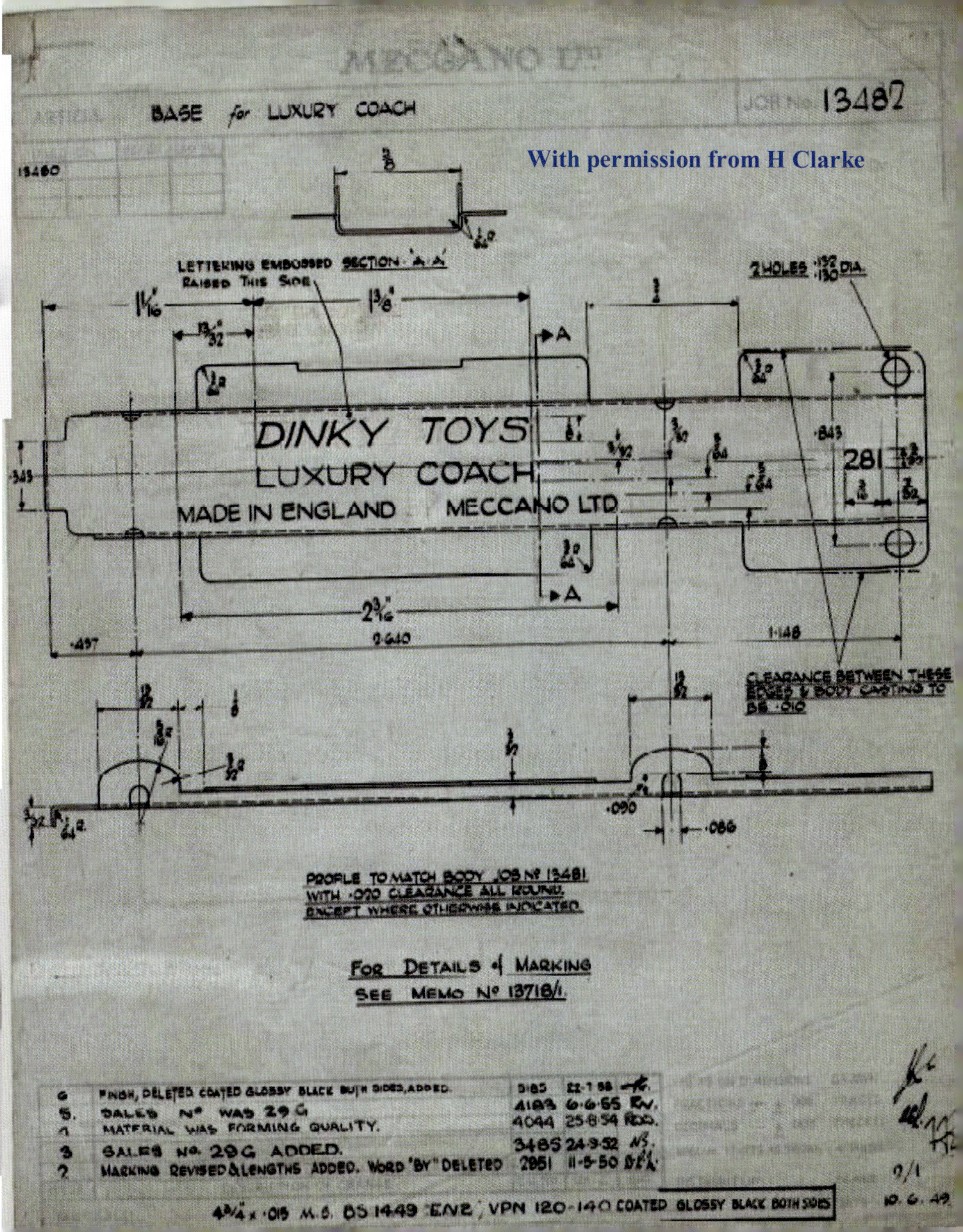

With permission from H Clarke

There were five basic colour schemes:
- maroon with cream flashes and either maroon or red wheel hubs - an original with white tyres has also recently been seen
- fawn with orange flashes and cream, green or red wheel hubs
- cream with orange flashes and cream, red or green wheel hubs - replaced the fawn in about 1956
- different shade of cream with red flashes and cream, green or red wheel hubs
- blue with cream flashes and cream wheels hub, probably first appeared in 1957

The rarer blue livery was also later used on the Duple Roadmaster Coach.

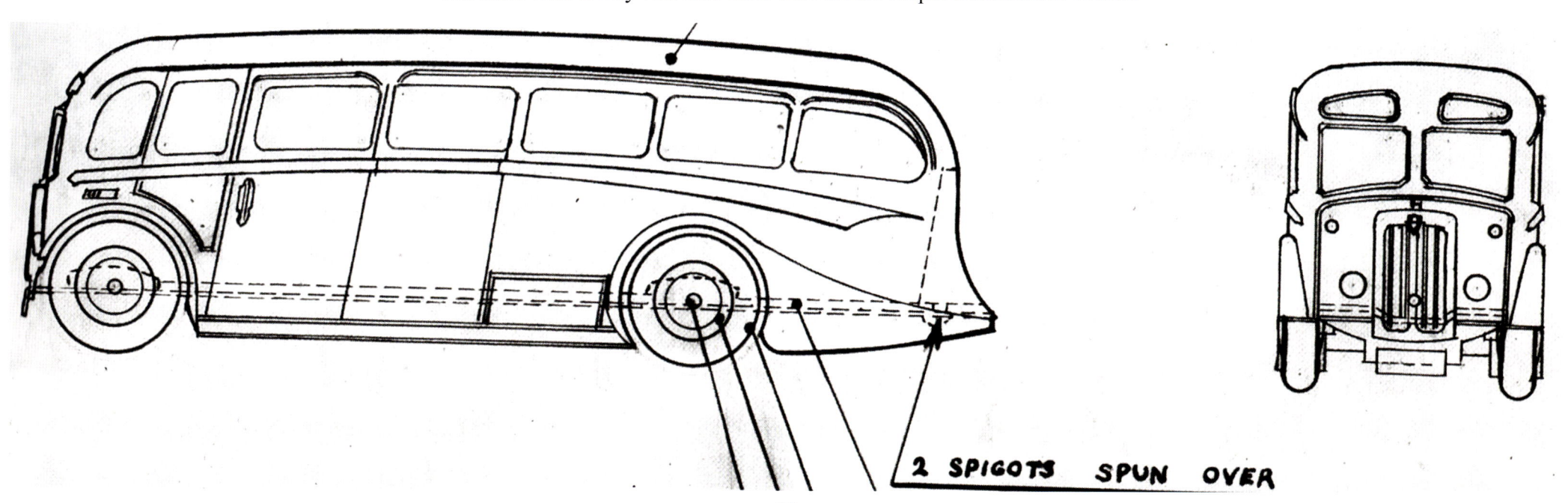

2 SPIGOTS SPUN OVER

The Luxury Coach was originally sold in a tradebox of six, replaced in 1954 with specific model boxes.

For less than a year the early boxes carried dual numbers on the end flap, to be replaced by a box with only the catalogue number 281 on the end flap and on the side.

The early boxes had a fawn image on one side and a maroon on the other. There was a printed colour spot on the end flap indicating which version the box contained. These boxes were later used to hold the blue buses, and hence came with an adhesive blue spot. Later boxes featured the blue variant and the cream coach with red wheels.

82

Observation Coach

The Observation Coach toy, was based on a Maudslay Marathon III with James Whitson coachwork, seating about 33 people.

This style of vehicle was intended for extended touring holidays and was popular from about 1948 to 1952. One was exhibited at the Commercial Motor Show in London in October 1948.

Such a vehicle won a silver cup and the Grand Prix d'Honneur at the second International Coach Concours at Nice in June 1949. The competition was arranged by an association of French Bodybuilders and some 47 entries from Belgium, France, Italy, Switzerland and Great Britain were received.

Another was exhibited at the 1950 New York Motor Show and received several awards plus an order from the United States Air Force, based on the Crossley chassis.

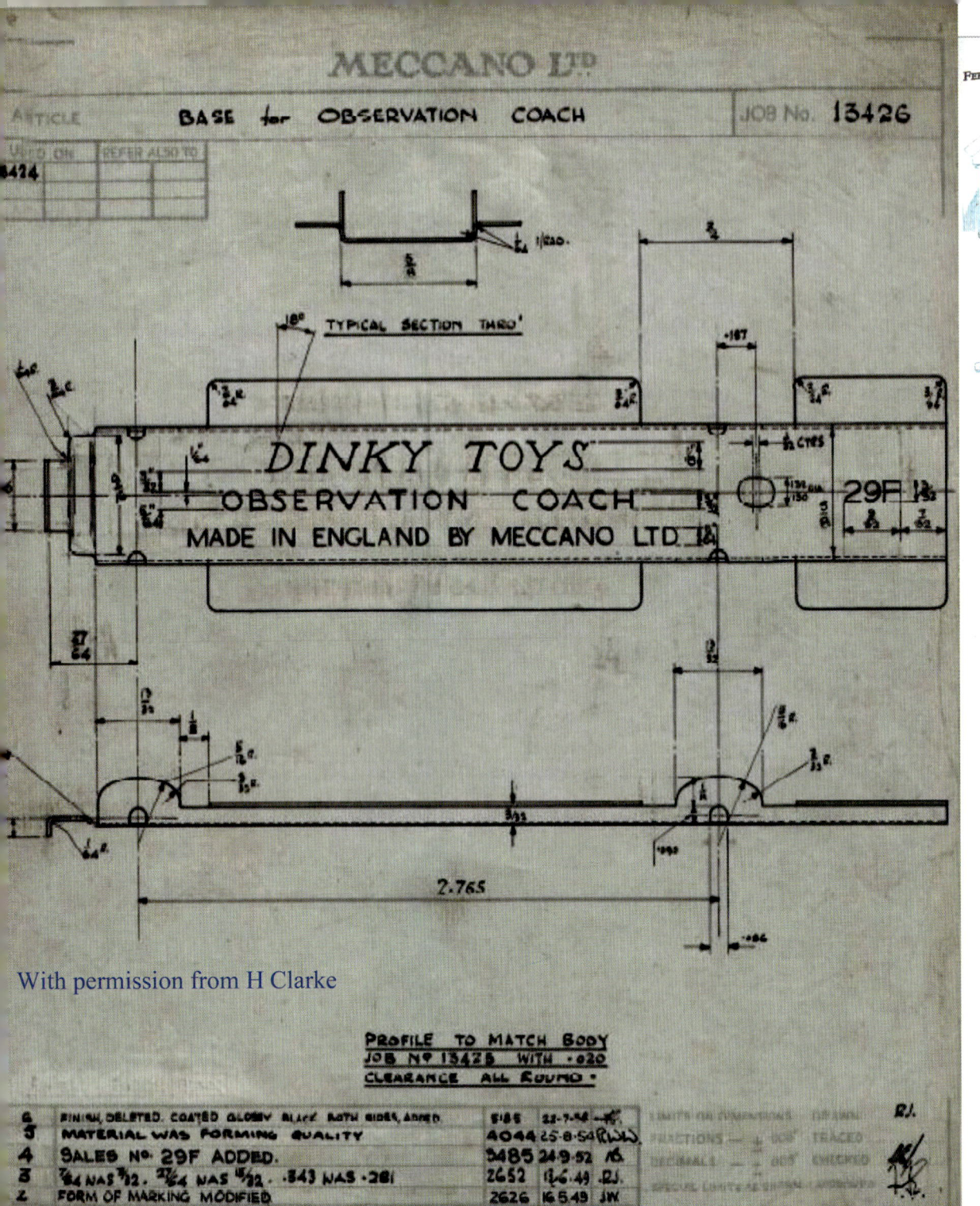

MECCANO LTD

ARTICLE: BASE for OBSERVATION COACH
JOB No. 13426

Drawing shows: DINKY TOYS / OBSERVATION COACH / MADE IN ENGLAND BY MECCANO LTD — 29F

PROFILE TO MATCH BODY
JOB N° 1342B WITH ·020
CLEARANCE ALL ROUND

6	FINISH, DELETED. COATED GLOSSY BLACK BOTH SIDES, ADDED	5185 22-7-56	
5	MATERIAL WAS FORMING QUALITY	4044 25-8-54	
4	SALES N° 29F ADDED	3485 24-9-52	
3	7/64 WAS 3/32. 27/64 WAS 13/32. ·543 WAS ·281	2652 13-6-49	
2	FORM OF MARKING MODIFIED	2626 16-5-49 JW	

With permission from H Clarke

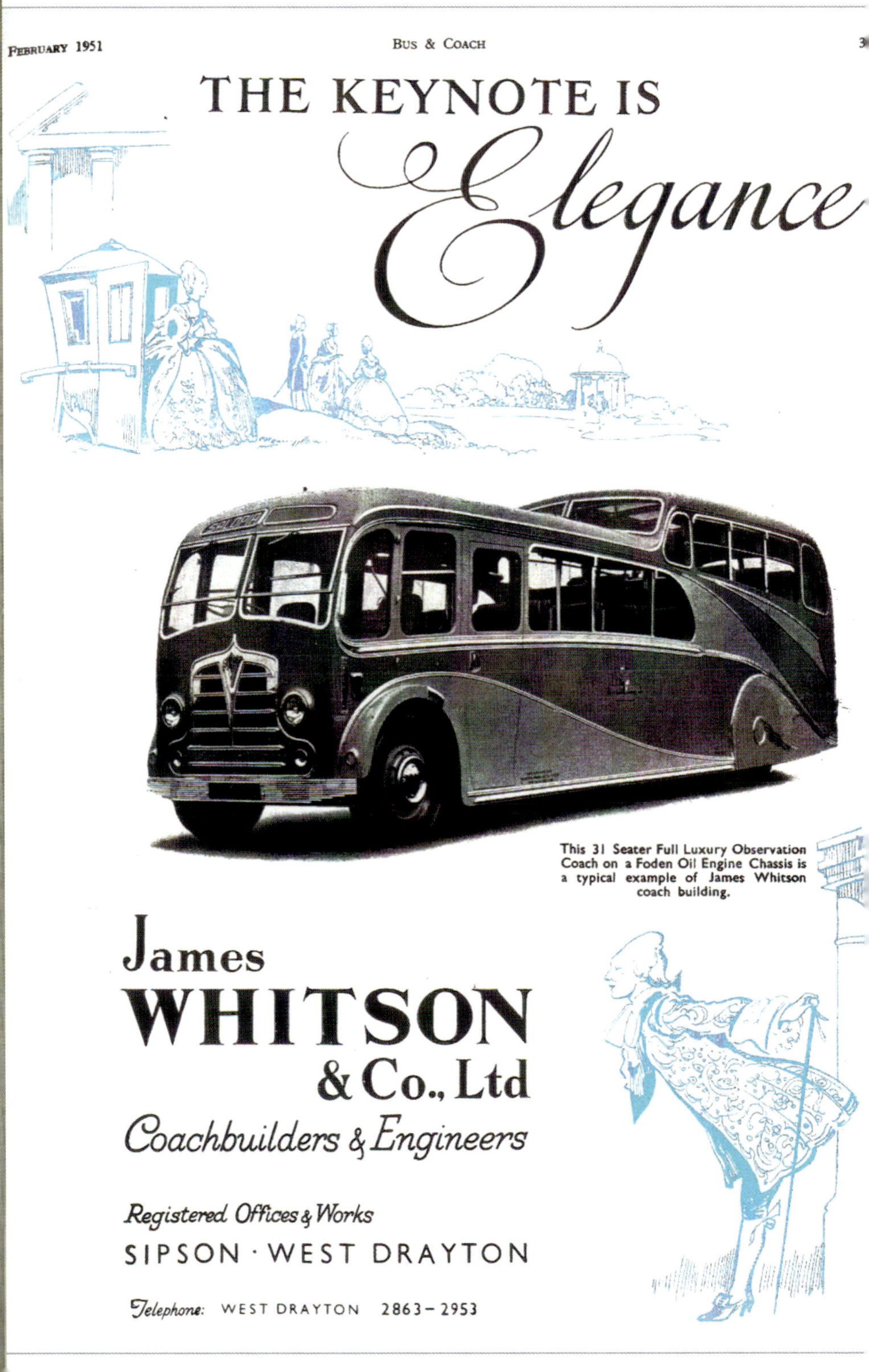

DATE 6·4·49

FEBRUARY 1951 — BUS & COACH

THE KEYNOTE IS *Elegance*

This 31 Seater Full Luxury Observation Coach on a Foden Oil Engine Chassis is a typical example of James Whitson coach building.

James **WHITSON** & Co., Ltd
Coachbuilders & Engineers

Registered Offices & Works

SIPSON · WEST DRAYTON

Telephone: WEST DRAYTON 2863–2953

The toy was in production from August 1950 until 1960. It was originally given catalogue number 29F but was later renumbered to 280.

There were only two basic colour schemes: grey with red flashes and either grey or red wheel hubs; cream with cream or red wheel hubs

The grey model has at least four different shades of grey. The two extremes being a dark grey and a green shaded grey. It's commonly believed, the darker the grey, the older the item.

The cream model with red wheels is the hardest to locate but were nevertheless made all the way through production of this item.

Early toys had red lights painted on the rear.

This toy was originally sold in a tradebox of six. By 1954 these were replaced by individual boxes.

During their first year, these individual boxes carried dual numbers on the end flap.

This was replaced by a box with only the catalogue number 280 on the end flap and an additional number on the side in a red oval with white figures.

The images on the sides showed the cream and grey models with a colour spot to indicate the specific colour variation contained in the box

Early box with dual numbers

86

The four different shades of grey of the Observation Coach.

Towards the end of production (1958 or 1959), the chassis was produced from a smoother metal and looked very different.

An Observation Coach with white tyres, which are rarely seen on this model.

Duple Roadmaster Coach

By the early 1950's the concept of the single-deck half-cab coach, which had originated in the 1930's, was fast disappearing. The real bus was based on a Leyland PSU1/15 Royal Tiger under-floor engine chassis, with a metal-framed body built by Duple. One was displayed at the 1950 Commercial Vehicle Show held at Earls Court, London.

The Duple Roadmaster coach was considered to be the last word in luxury, possessing some novel features for the time: forty-one luxurious individual adjustable seats, cushioned with double density latex rubber and mounted on pedestals with tubular footrests; the rear luggage compartment had a capacity of 80-85 cubic feet and was fitted with an automatic light!; the interior was lit by short fluorescent tubes, which were considered quite something in those days.

An unusual feature was a spare-wheel housing in the front of the body.

The staff at Duple nicknamed them 'Iron Dukes'.

There has been a suggestion that this vehicle, with its modern lines, might have appealed more to the North American market, being similar in style to many vehicles entering service across the Atlantic at the time.

It is now considered more likely to have been copied from vehicles brought into service in South America.

Production only lasted for a year or so and one could say that the vehicle enjoyed a much longer life as a Dinky Toy than it did on the road!

MECCANO LTD

ARTICLE: BASE for DUPLE ROADMASTER TOURING COACH   **JOB No.** 13752

With permission from H Clarke

DUPLE
at Earls Court ..

A superb new luxury coach and the latest type of double deck bus—two of the models that will be representing the range and versatility of Duple coachbuilding at the Commercial Motor Show, Earls Court. For design and performance each is outstanding in its class, worthy of the great traditions of Duple craftsmanship.

Duple "Roadmaster" metal-framed luxury coach, suitable for under-floor engine chassis. 41 or more seats. Many new features, including latest type Duple inward folding entrance door. Designed for use in Great Britain and overseas.

Coachbuilders to

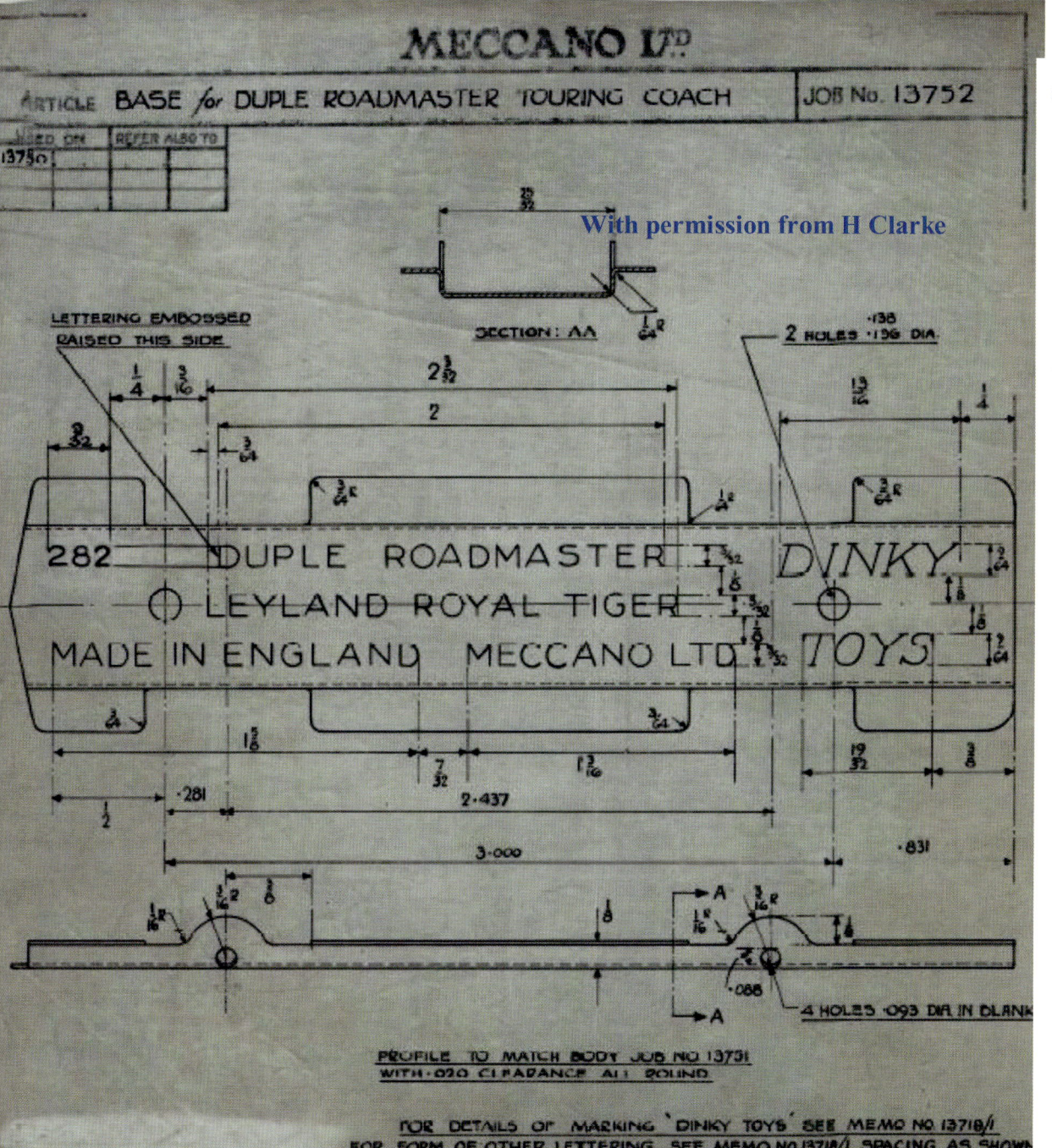

DUPLE MOTOR BODIES LIMITED

The toy was first issued in September 1952 under catalogue number 29H and renumbered 282 in 1954. At about the same time the single deck half-cab bus was discontinued and so this model could be regarded as a replacement.

There are no known external variations to the body. The interior roof was originally smooth but modified less than six months into production by the introduction of a rib running from front to back, *probably to aid the flow of molten mazak (zinc alloy) to the extremities of the rivet spigot casting.*

Towards the end of its production life, cross-hatched line patterns were added to the inside of the roof, the purpose behind which is unknown but the assumption is that it was an added feature to aid the casting being ejected from the tooling. Most of the yellow toys and a few of the red ones found so far contain this particular casting change.

The only other casting changes were to the chassis, as the catalogue number was not initially carried, but it has been seen on blue, red and yellow toys. In the last couple of years of production the chassis was made from a smoother metal and looks very different from the earlier models.

The first toy appeared in red and blue liveries with silver grill and trim surrounding the entire vehicle. A two-tone variant in green/cream was added to the range, probably around the middle of 1953, with the aim of attracting the North American market. It had wheel hubs in cream, green or red, although the green and red versions are difficult to find.

A much rarer version was produced in a paler blue, and it is possible that it was part of a limited run, and may have been simply to use up paint left over from a previous model. These models were probably made in the middle of the 1950's.

PUBLIC SERVICE VEHICLES — DINKY TOYS — PUBLIC SERVICE VEHICLES

282
Duple Roadmaster Coach
Length 4¾"
3/5

290
Double Deck Bus DUNLOP
Length 4"
4/2

295
Atlas Bus (Standard Atlas Kenebrake)
(with windows, steering wheel, seating and four-wheel suspension)
Length 3⅜"   3/9

291
London Bus EXIDE   Length 4"
4/2

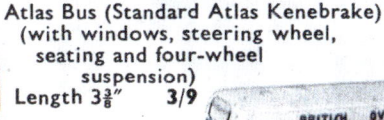

283
B.O.A.C. Coach   Length 4¾"
4/2

This is a rather "odd" casting that I found. There is an extra pillar in the rear window. There appears to be no explanation for this.

TRANSPORT WORLD, November 4, 1950

ANOTHER TRIUMPH FOR DUPLE...

The Roadmaster Coach

Duple "Roadmaster" metal-framed luxury coach, suitable for underfloor engine chassis. 41/45 seats.

THIS superb new coach typifies the forward policy of Duple designers. Suitable for underfloor engine chassis, it is styled throughout for luxurious comfort and smooth performance. The many new features include the latest type Duple inward folding entrance door. Duple craftsmanship keeps true to form with "Roadmaster"!

Also available—the new "Ambassador" Streamlined Super Luxury Coach!

We are pleased to announce that our Repair and Service Department is now reopened for repairs and renovations to all coachwork.

DUPLE

Coachbuilders to the world

DUPLE MOTOR BODIES LTD., THE HYDE, HENDON, LONDON, N.W.9

By 1957, a yellow toy with red trim appeared. This clearly looked like an American school bus, which is probably why it proved so popular in the USA. This might have also been the reason for the later introduction of the Wayne School Bus in order that Dinky might capture the US market. *This example is hard to find in pure, mint condition because the yellow paint seems to chip very easily.* The wheel hubs of this version are normally yellow, but other colours exist including red and green.

Towards the end of production white tyres replaced the black and this mix can be found on both the red and yellow liveries.

There is also in existence a rather interesting prototype in red/cream which was sold at auction a number of years ago. *Who knows what else might be out there!*

This model has proved very popular for using on model railway layouts because it is close to the scale of 1:76.

92

They were originally sold in tradeboxes but by 1954, individual boxes were being issued. A few of the early examples had dual numbers although these were quickly replaced by boxes bearing just the catalogue number 282 on the end flaps.

Initially the box carried a red image of the model on one side and blue on the other. However within three years the blue was replaced by the yellow model.

Much later this toy was sold in plain boxes with alternate red and yellow sides, *but they are difficult to find.*

The catalogue number appears on the end flaps and on the sides of the boxes. The side number was later changed to a red oval with white numbers which is found on boxes with the red and yellow images as well as boxes with red and blue images.

The end flap usually carried the colour spot associated with the colour of the model inside *and* yes, for the avoidance of doubt, boxes with yellow spots do exist.

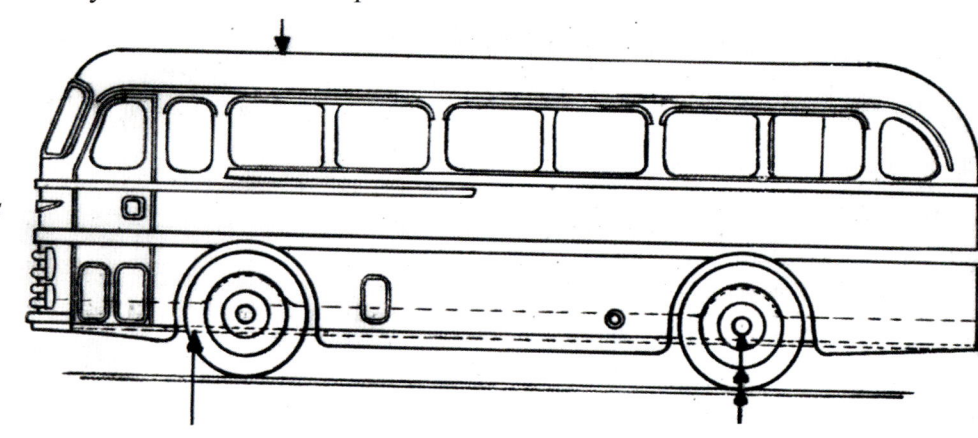

Toys, aimed at the North American market, displaying the different coloured wheel hubs

95

A line up of 4 buses in the Dinky range, all in the lighter blue colour - giving an interesting comparison between them.

BOAC Coach

The vehicle used in service by BOAC had Commer running-gear and a body produced by Thomas Harrington which was known as the Contender. This was a chassisless design using aluminium construction. Early ones had the same petrol engine as the Commer Avenger, while later models had a two-stroke TS3 diesel engine.

BOAC bought 12 such coaches between 1953 and 1958, the last three having Rolls-Royce petrol engines and automatic transmission. One was on display at the 1952 Earls Court Commercial Motor Show and had 35 seats and ample rear luggage space.

The vehicle on which the model is based was unusual in having a central passenger entrance with an outward-opening entrance door.

The toy was released in October 1956 and remained in production until 1963. It had a catalogue number of 283.

Although the toy was produced for seven years there were no casting changes. The only alteration was to the chassis, which was modified from a rough to a smooth metal. This probably happened mid-way through the production cycle.

97

Aluminium...
...Chassisless

First in the field of genuinely chassisless passenger vehicles this de-luxe motor coach is the product of Messrs. Thomas Harrington Ltd. In collaboration with the Development Department of the British Aluminium Company which supplied all the aluminium, Harringtons have developed this vehicle which features many advantages. The unladen weight of the complete vehicle compares favourably with the bare chassis weight of a standard-type underfloor engined chassis. A seating arrangement for 41 passengers has been achieved allowing ample room for luggage. The mechanised components are easily accessible and are of Commer origin.

British Aluminium

THE BRITISH ALUMINIUM CO LTD · NORFOLK HOUSE · ST JAMES'S SQUARE · LONDON SW1

NOVEMBER 1952   Bus & Coach

STRENGTH
with *Lightness*

The vehicle illustrated above is the Commer Harrington 'Contender' 41-seater chassisless Coach. The unladen weight of this vehicle is 4.13.3.0. Commer mechanical components are used with Commer 109 B.H.P. engine, mounted forward of the front axle. The prototype illustrated above will shortly be demonstrated in selected areas of the British Isles.

HARRINGTON
COACHWORK
HOVE

THOMAS HARRINGTON LIMITED · SACKVILLE WORKS · HOVE · ENGLAND · *Telephone* HOVE

In general the toy captures the appearance of the real vehicle except for the lower front windows, which should have been glass.

Only two types of presentation boxes were used:
1. the standard yellow box with a picture of the coach on the side
2. the box that had alternate yellow and red sides

The tyres were originally plain black and knobbly and were replaced by a white tyre version in 1960.

Spun wheels were added in 1962 towards the end of the production life.

The livery was always the same blue with a white roof and carrying stylish fleetnames along the sides.

Atlas Bus

The toy was based on the 948 cc Standard Atlas Kenebrake 12-seater built by the Kenex company. It was their habit to take delivery of the normal Standard Atlas panel van originally with a 948cc engine and apply the necessary customised conversions. The original engine and running gear came from the 1954-60 Standard Ten / Standard Pennant models. The later 1670 cc engine came from the 1957-61 Standard Ensign, and this was superseded by a 2138cc engine.

The toy was announced in the May 1960 issue of the Meccano Magazine, which carried an advertisement for it on the back page.

The catalogue number was 295. Initially the livery was blue/grey and later an all-over light-blue toy was added.

Facing competition from Corgi, whose attention to detail in their toys was very precise, Dinky wanted to ensure this new miniature vehicle looked good. It was supplied with interior seat details in red and was one of their first toy buses to have plastic windows. Exterior details included steps on the nearside and at the rear. It also had suspension, giving it more 'play value' than many of their previous toys.

Production lasted from 1960 to 1964, *quite a short life for what seemed like a very attractive item.*

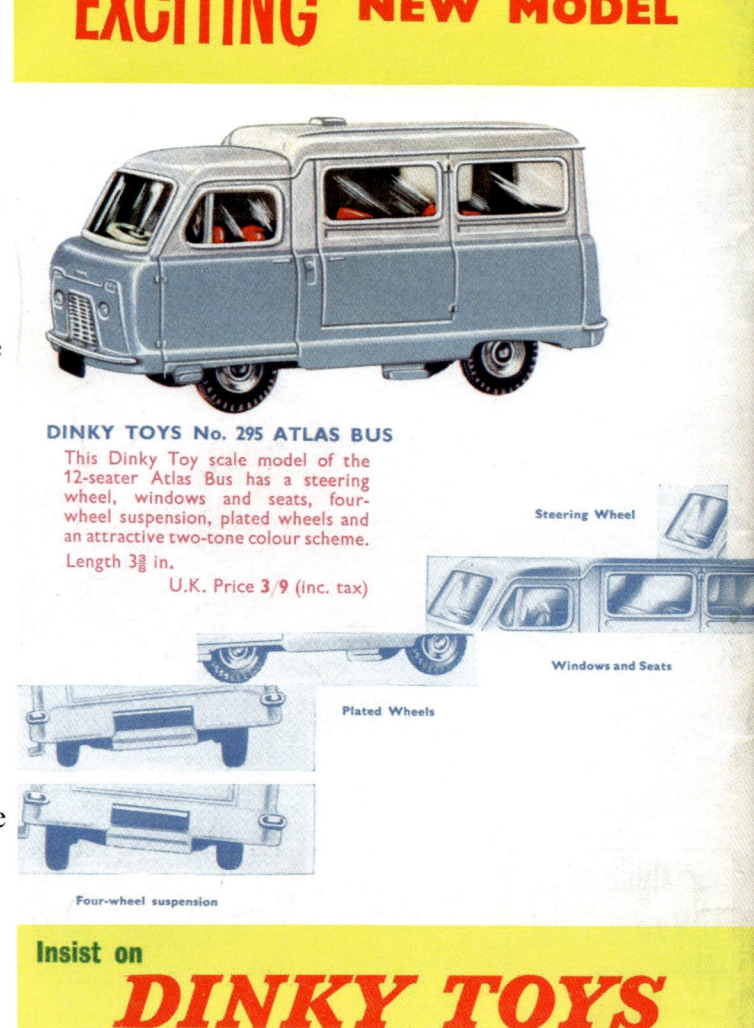

100

The only 2 colour variants of the Dinky model.

Nicky diecast toy

The Atlas Bus was sold in two types of presentation boxes: the standard yellow box with an artists impression of the bus on the side and the box that had alternate yellow and red sides

Towards the end of its production life it appeared as one of six items in the Touring Gift set under catalogue number 122. This set was only produced for about a year and also contained: the Rambler Station Wagon and caravan, a Jaguar 3.4, a Healey sports boat on trailer and an AA Motorcycle Patrol.

A few years later the mould was used in India as part of the Nicky range of diecast toys, along with a number of other Dinky vehicles.

There are many colour variations, but the above is the version most similar to Dinky. The only real difference being in the quality of the finished product.

101

Wayne School Bus / Continental Touring Coach

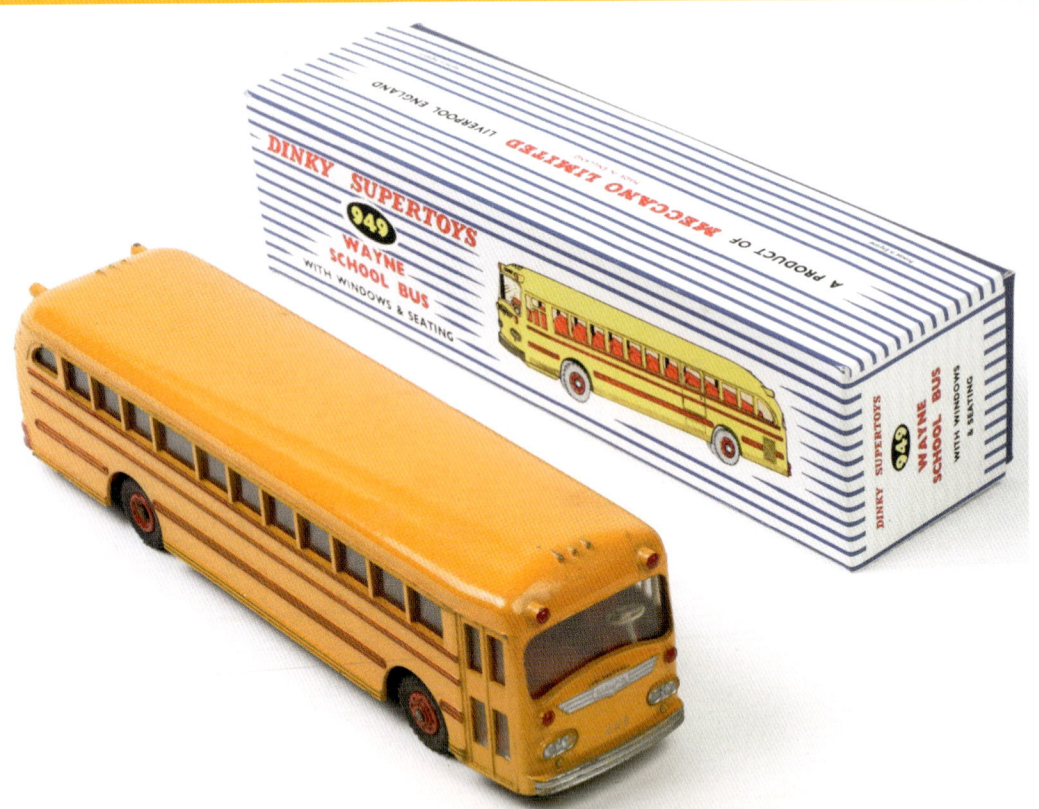

Based on the Wayne Superamic Transit Coach, manufactured by the Wayne Divco-Wayne Corporation based in Richmond, Indiana, USA. It was a little different from many of the dedicated school buses in America because most were bonneted, but for a number of years Wayne produced a full-front version.

The first mention of this American-style bus was in the February 1961 issue of Meccano Magazine, which also carried an advertisement on the back page.

The catalogue number was 949 in the Dinky Supertoys range and production lasted until 1964.

It's 8¾ inches in length, with plastic windows and interior details, with red seats but surprisingly no suspension.

The livery was the standard American school bus deep yellow with small details highlighted in either silver or appropriate colours for the light clusters. 'School Bus' is normally found on the front and rear plus 'unlawful to pass when loading or unloading'. Initially, the lines along the sides were red but a later variation had black lines.

The presentation box was either the blue and white stripes variety or the yellow box.

Continental Touring Coach

In 1963 a version with a livery of turquoise with a white roof and seats in a light tan was produced, to appeal to a wider audience.

'Dinky Continental Tours' was printed in red on a white background along the roof.

There was also a minor change to the chassis to indicate the different bus.

The catalogue number was 953 and it was in production for two years.

The casting later appeared in India in the Nicky range of diecast toys, probably around 1970, but few of those seem to have been made

103

Holidays abroad by motor coach

The Continental Touring Coach was featured in the January 1963 issue of Meccano Magazine along with an advertisement on the back page.
The Wayne School Bus was on the front cover.

DINKY TOYS No. 953—CONTINENTAL TOURING COACH

Paris, Rome, Brussels, Vienna . . . all these cities, and many more, are visited every year by hundreds of coaches similar to the prototype of this Dinky Supertoy. The model itself is fitted with specially tinted windows, seats and steering wheel and is finished in a delightful pale blue gloss with white roof. The words "Dinky Continental Tours" appear on each side.
Length 8¾ in. U.K. Price 13/6

The last word in realism!

DINKY TOYS No. 277 SUPERIOR CRITERION AMBULANCE WITH FLASHING LIGHT

With siren wailing and roof-light flashing the ambulance rushes its patient to hospital! This striking miniature also is fitted with a red roof-light which actually flashes as the vehicle is pushed along. Realistic figures of driver and attendant occupy the front seats. These refinements are additional to the regular Dinky Toys features:— Prestomatic steering, windows, suspension and seats.
Length 5 in. U.K. Price 8/9
Battery No. 036 (Vidor V16) is not supplied with the model, but may be purchased separately. Price 5d.

DINKY TOYS MADE BY MECCANO LTD.

AVAILABLE LATER OVERSEAS

Published by MECCANO LTD., Binns Road, Liverpool 13, England. Printed by John Waddington Ltd., Leeds & London

DINKY TOYS GIVE LASTING PLEASURE

H. SALANSON & CO. LTD.
83-85 Fairfax Street
BRISTOL, 1

A 737 P.1.B. Lightning Fighter 2¼" — 56 mm. (Wing Span)

G 955 Fire Engine with Extending Ladder 5½" — 140 mm.

M 953 Continental Touring Coach 8¾" — 222 mm.

M 952 Vega Major Luxury Coach 9⅝" — 245 mm.

B 257 Fire Chief's Car 4" — 102 mm.

M 908 Mighty Antar with Transformer 13¼" — 337 mm.

M 949 Wayne School Bus 8¾" — 222 mm.

H 944 SHELL B.P. Fuel Tanker 7⅝" — 194 mm.

M 989 Car Carrier 9½" — 243 mm.

MORE FEATURES:—
★ SAFETY BELTS · DETACHABLE "TOPS"
★ JEWELLED LIGHTS · DRIVERS

7/164/450   MECCANO LIMITED, LIVERPOOL   Printed in England

Vega Major Luxury Coach

The Bedford VAL chassis was a twin-steer design. This was not something new because during the late 1930's and early 1940's, Leyland had built small numbers of single-deck twin-steer Gnu & Panda models. Following a few twin-steer versions of the Tiger and a change in Ministry of Transport regulations which permitted a 30 foot chassis on two axles, the idea was quickly dropped.

Vauxhall launched it afresh, with a 36 foot chassis at the 1962 Commercial Motor Show in London. Originally fitted with the Leyland O.400 straight six-diesel engine. The chassis was designated as a VAL14 and at a price of £1775 it was about £1000 cheaper than a Leyland or AEC equivalent. It was also a ton lighter and having an average fuel consumption of around 15mpg.

The VAL was built with bodies supplied by various coachbuilders. The majority were of Duple or Plaxton origin, although there were some Harrington and Yeates.

The Bedford VAL was used in the original Michael Caine version of The Italian Job. The actual vehicle being a Harrington Legionnaire. A Plaxton-bodied Val was used in the 1967 Beatles' film, Magical Mystery Tour.

Production of the VAL ceased in 1973, by which time 2000 or more had been built. No other manufacturer has since produced a twin-steer PSV design, although twin rear-axle designs are common.

The toy, which was based on the Bedford Val with a Duple body was featured and advertised in the December 1963, January 1964 and March 1964 issues of the Meccano Magazine.

It was called a 'Vega Major Luxury Coach' with no mention of the Bedford or Duple names. The original catalogue number was 952. The toy had windows, seats and suspension. New features for Dinky included: independently flashing amber indicators; twin front-steering axles with Prestomatic steering on each, and an opening boot, the first on a Supertoy.

This advert has an incorrect catalogue number for the Vega Major Luxury Coach

The Vega Major Luxury Coach was produced between 1964 and 1971.

Early versions came with an instruction sheet explaining how to change the light bulbs, which could be purchased separately.

In 1971, the toy was re-catalogued as 954 because the amber flashing indicators had been removed which meant that there was no need for a battery compartment in the chassis. The indicators were now clear plastic.

106

VAL

The great new 52/55 seater by **BEDFORD**

Radically new COMFORT, SAFETY, ECONOMY

The livery was cream, with the shade changing over the years. The second colour was in fact a "sticker".

The seat colours:
- Initially cream
- then came blue (at least two different shades)
- towards the end of production and rarer, they were either yellow or red.

Different shades of cream livery

Older toy with amber flashing indicators

Later toy with yellow seats and clear indicators

Later toy with red seats and clear indicators

107

Between 1973 and 1977, an additional export version was produced in the Swiss PTT colours of yellow, cream and red, with a specific catalogue number of 961.
None were sold in the UK.
They usually had blue plastic windows but there are some with yellow. Frequently the interior seats were two shades of blue, but yellow seats have also been seen.

Box styles for the Vega Major Luxury Coach:
1. Strong lift-up top with an image of a mountain road and stating Dinky Supertoy
2. More flimsy with a seaside scene in the background
3. Featured an actual photo of the toy
4. Export version is more colourful and stated that it was a 'Swiss Postal Bus'. There was an additional version of the box in red and white with PTT in large letters along the sides
5. Card-tray with a clear plastic cover, easily damaged appeared mid 1970's

Recently an interesting version has come to light, a see through box with cardboard end flaps announcing it as the 'Vega Major Luxury Touring Coach'. This model was produced for export sales, but the box is very flimsy and few have survived.

One other box in which this wonderful toy appeared was the Holiday Gift Set which was produced between 1964 and 1967, had catalogue number 124 and consisted of 4 vehicles.

So, in total, this model appeared in 8 different styles of packaging, if the catalogue number change is included, more than almost any other Dinky Toys model.

Luxury Coach

The Duple Viceroy 37 body was introduced at the 1968 Commercial Motor Show in London after a few had already entered service. The number 37, indicated the length, in feet, of the vehicle. The chassis was produced by any one of a number of manufacturers, including Bedford, Ford and Leyland.

This vehicle was an update on the standard Viceroy body, with the frontal appearance being redesigned to incorporate a new stainless steel front grille with headlamps below, which are enclosed by a toughened panel.

The toy, with catalogue number 296, was announced in the July 1972 Meccano Magazine, with an advert stating recommended retail price of 32 pence and a brief glimpse in the May issue.

Production lasted for about four years.

It was well detailed on the outside with speedwheels. The interior had basic plastic seats which look a little oversized for the model.

The livery was metallic blue and the plastic windows were tinted orange but some were clear.

Unlike some of their later buses it had no gimmicks. However the scale was very different from other buses produced by Dinky over the years. It's probably nearer to TT scale.

109

A second colour variant followed in 1973, yellow/cream for the Swiss PTT with catalogue number 293. For the first three years it was sold in Switzerland, but later was available elsewhere. The plastic windows were tinted blue, but there were some with orange tinted or clear windows. Production continued until about 1978.

This colour variation has always been popular, with many miniature buses produced in it over the years.

296 Luxury Coach WITH SPEEDWHEELS   NEW for '72

119 mm.

355 Lunar Roving Vehicle

Front and Rear Wheels steered by pivoting central control column. Model Astronauts. Simulated Solar Energy Cells.

114 mm.

The Luxury Coach was boxed in a card tray with a clear lid sitting on a deep base.

The Swiss PTT card tray box also came with a plastic lid, with later versions having a shallower base. The bases clearly state 'Swiss PTT Bus'.

I bought a Swiss PTT Bus in 1979 for 99 pence. How times have changed!

Single Decker Bus

In 1966 London Transport instigated a 'Bus Reshaping Plan' to examine bus services in London. As a result of this a decision was made to replace some double-decker buses with 36 foot long standee single-decker rear-engined buses.

They were designed for one-man-operation (OMO) and had separate entrance and exit doors to speed up passenger flow.

The seating in the bus was sufficient to meet off-peak demand but provided plenty of room for standing passengers during peak times.

The single decker bus was introduced in London on 18 April 1966, with 6 AEC Merlin buses used on a new express service, Route 500, the famous 'Red Arrow', running between Victoria and Marble Arch, a route which was extended during shopping hours as far as Oxford Circus.

The toy first appeared in 1971, with an advertisement on the back of the May 1971 Meccano Magazine. The list of special features stated: capacity for 72 passengers; moulded seats which were initially blue and later yellow; a steering wheel; bell and automatic doors.

The catalogue number was 283, like the earlier BOAC coach.

Early toys were painted in metallic red, with red passenger doors and a cream chassis.

The livery then changed to a more 'normal' red, with cream/ white doors.

White stickers, as opposed to transfers, were applied along the sides bearing the name 'Red Arrow' and carrying the familiar London Transport bullseye.

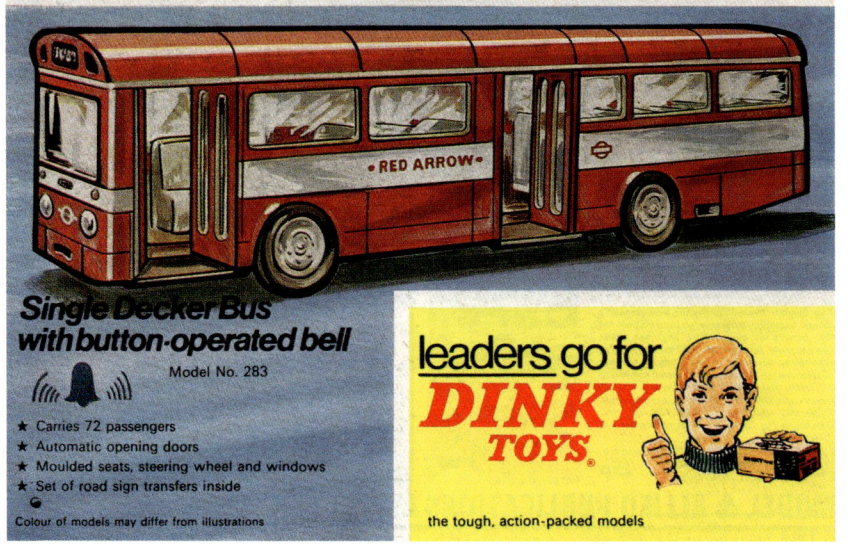

The early toys came in yellow boxes with a white sticker on the sides which announced two exciting features: automatically opening doors and a button-operated bell. The end flap indicated it was a 'Single Decker Bus'. Each box came with stickers and an instruction sheet.

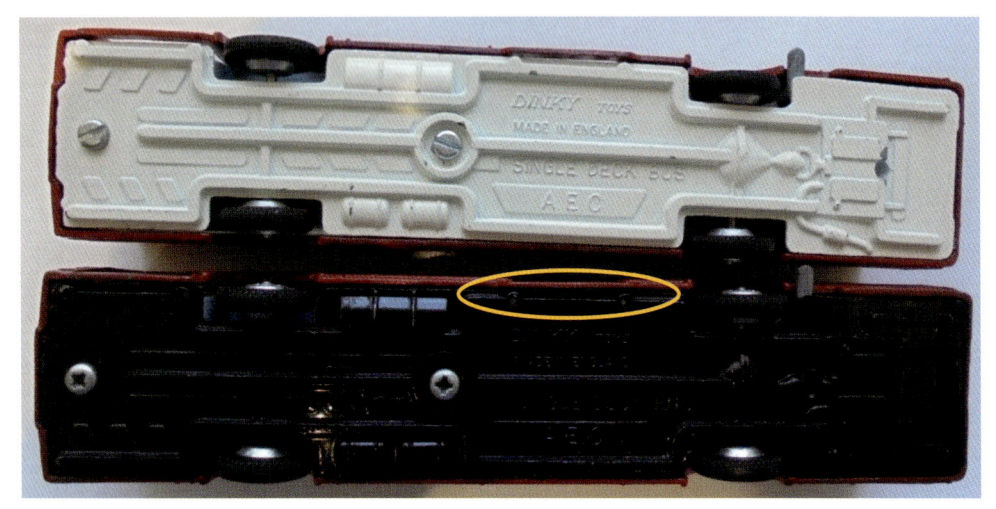

The cream chassis was later replaced by a black chassis with a minor casting change: two holes had been inserted on the edge above DINKY TOYS. Also crosshead screws were used instead of slotted.

112

Later packaging was the card tray type with a clear plastic lid of which there are two versions. The earlier and rarer, has a much deeper base, similar to the early Luxury Coach. The description along the sides of the box has 'Single Decker Bus' on one line and '283' on a second line. The later and better known shallow base box, has 'Single Decker Bus' and '283' on the same line.

'Action Kits' were first introduced in the May 1971 Meccano Magazine. The article announced a new range of construction kits based on the model vehicles currently available in the Dinky range. A full-page black-and-white advertisement for the single decker bus kit, appeared in the April 1972 Meccano Magazine. The June and July issues carried a full-page colour advertisement on the back page showing the assembled kit painted green.

A kit version with catalogue number 1023 was packaged in a book-type box. It opened out to reveal the full casting and 32 items including a bottle of green paint. Full instructions were on the inside. Stickers provided were for 'Green Line' to match the paint.

The '*other version*' is a toy in a green livery. There is no information regarding the green version as having been officially produced by Dinky, but toys have been offered for sale. The shades of green differ, while headlamps are silver or green. *So possibly produced from the kits sold by the company.*

See 'Planned Section' for the toy in a green London Country livery advert.

Planned but never produced

These models were planned but never reached production for unknown reasons:

- Single Deck Bus (1934)
- 29 Motor Bus (1934)
- 247 London Transport E1 Tram 1975
- 248 Continental Tourer April 1978
- 248 Leyland National Lifeliner Casualty Unit 1975
- 249 Leyland National Midland Red 1975
- 292 AEC Merlin London Country 1977
- 250 Moscow Trolleybus 1980 Olympics 1977
- 628 Atlas Bus (military version)
- 950 Double Deck Bus

Paperweight produced for the London Toy Museum

The first was in the 1930's, when besides a double deck AEC Q, there were also plans to produce a single deck version. The drawings were produced but no prototype is believed to have been made.

Many years later the London Toy Museum produced a paperweight of this suggested model.

Not long after this the Model Shop Allsorts produced a small batch of the actual toy itself which were sold to collectors.

Precision Cast Models produced for Model Shop Allsorts

Paperweights produced for the London Toy Museum

A prototype for the Continental Tourer coach with a catalogue number of 248 was made and used in the last catalogue printed. Scale 1:76.

It's been suggested that a series of these might have been produced in a variety of football team colours, but only one known prototype seems to exist.

284 London Taxi 112mm

278 Plymouth Yellow Cab 134·5mm

248 Continental Tourer Coach 164·5 mm
Available in alternative Football club Liveries.

289 Routemaster London Bus 121mm

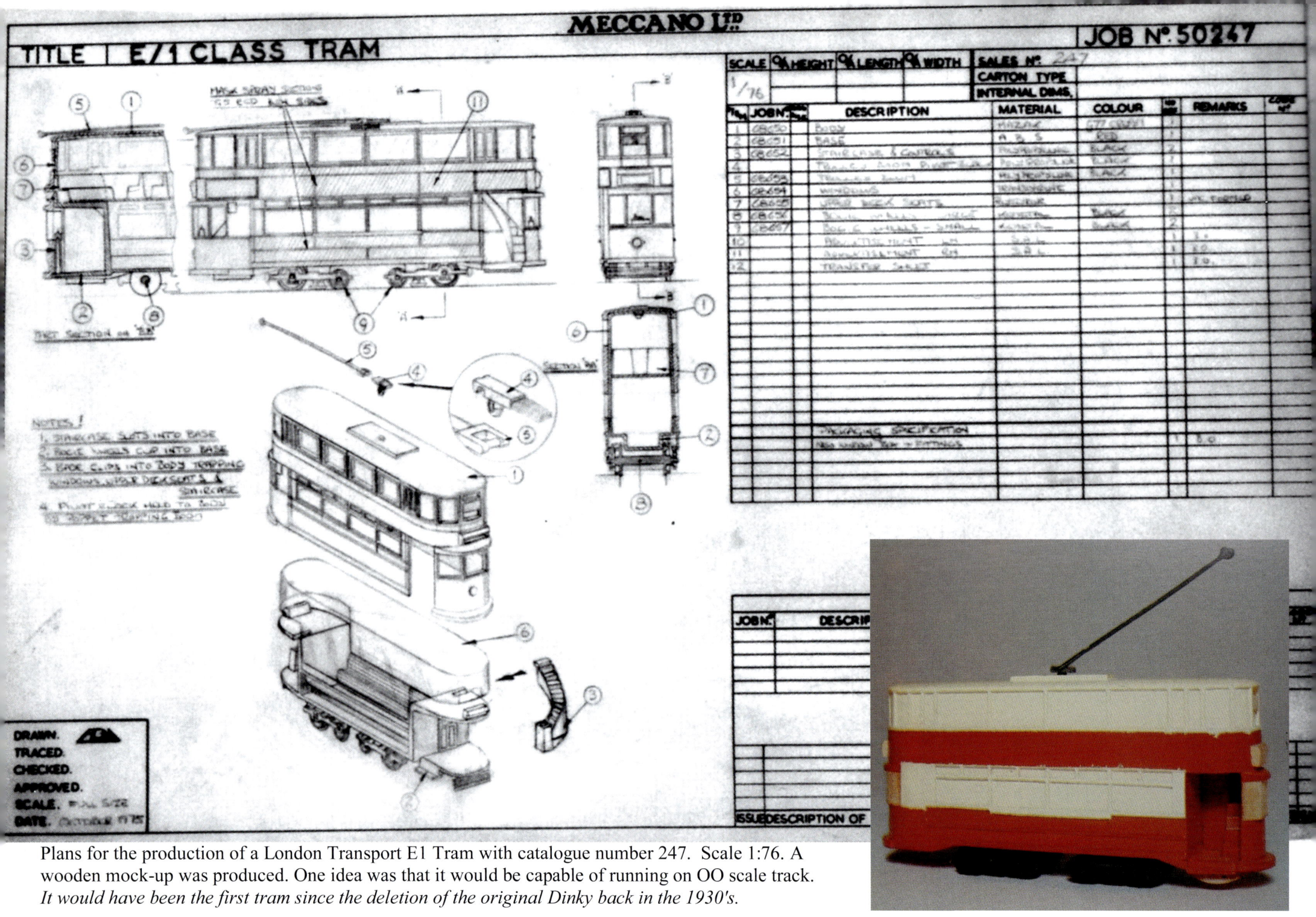

Plans for the production of a London Transport E1 Tram with catalogue number 247. Scale 1:76. A wooden mock-up was produced. One idea was that it would be capable of running on OO scale track. *It would have been the first tram since the deletion of the original Dinky back in the 1930's.*

1975 plan for Leyland National Lifeliner Casualty Unit. Catalogue number 248. Scale 1:76

It is unknown if 248 or 249 ever reached the prototype stage. Scale was 1:76

1975 plan for Leyland National Midland Red. Catalogue number 249. Scale 1:76

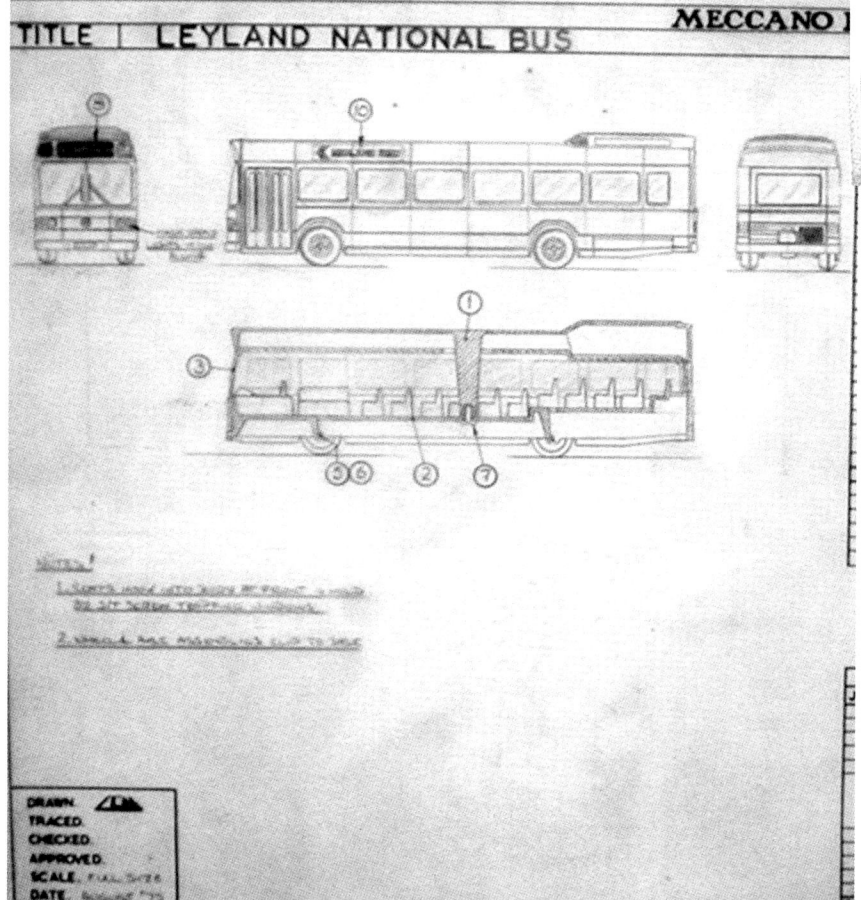

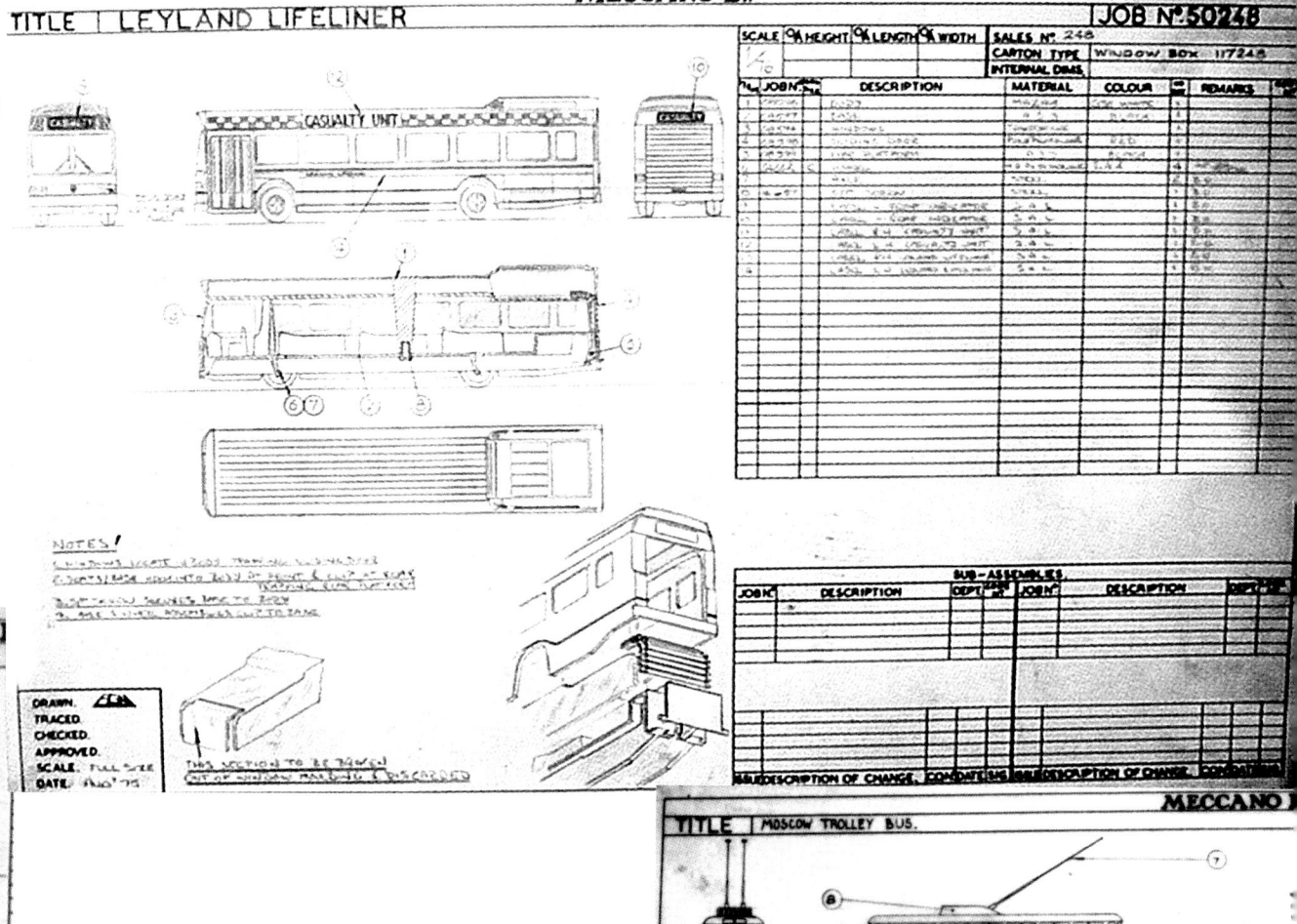

1977 plan for a Moscow trolleybus with 1980 Olympic decals. Catalogue number 250. Scale unknown

Unknown if an actual prototype was ever produced, possibly unlikely.

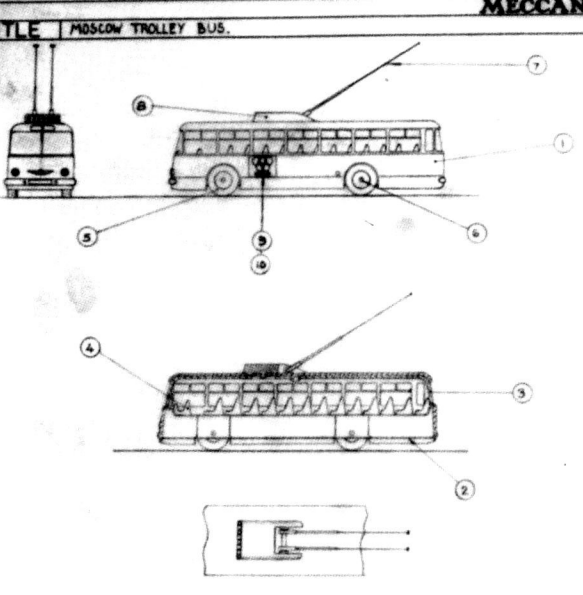

This catalogue has an advert for the AEC Merlin London Country 1977 with catalogue number 292

A trial livery on the **Duple Roadmaster Coach** that was never progressed and only one example is known to exist.

Diecast Copies

Streamlined Bus

Copies of this vehicle are rare, but one known example was produced in New Zealand by a company called Tink-E-Toys. *(Say the name out loud; it's as close to copyright infringement as is possible).*

This was a lead-cast copy, but with the addition of a fender, a single windscreen, and either solid-side or cut-out windows.

Photographs from E Diamond

Luxury Coach

For many years Morgan Milton of India made a diecast copy of the Luxury Coach from the original moulds. The base stated it was 'Luxury Coach - A Milton Product', which is a clear reference to its origins. At first it was a good copy, but the wheels were later replaced by speedwheels and the quality deteriorated drastically with each passing year.

The livery was cream with a red flash and the words 'Luxury Coach' appeared over the sliding door. The shade of cream becoming richer further into production. Early examples have been seen with some rather "sick looking" passengers inside. Some can be found in boxes marked 'Mini Auto Cars' with 'Luxury Coach' emblazoned on the sides.

A Milton Mini Toys catalogue shows that the company produced a vast range of diecast toys originating from a variety of English manufacturers including Dinky, Corgi, Budgie and Matchbox, together with a number of mainland European manufacturers.

A favourite description of the importance of a toy comes from a sister manufacturer called Maxwell, who also promoted a range of diecast vehicles. Maxwell described it thus: *'A toy is a model of the grown up world, scaled to the size of a child and needing a child's creativity to make it an object of play'*. Now that is a difficult description to beat!

No.	Name
814	Petrol Tanker
862	Highway Racer
817	Timber Transporter
813	Royal Mail
828	Circus Van
851	Air Line Bus
826	Mercedes Truck with Box
808	Mercedes Truck
806	Solid Car USA Fire Bird
820	New Model Ambulance
822	New Model School Bus
816	Luxury Coach
809	Mercends Truck with Logs
807	Plymouth Red Cross Amb.
860	Mini Double Decker

Pages from their catalogue clearly showing an image of the Dinky Luxury Coach copy, plus a few other exotic items.

122

Observation Coach

A very good copy of the Observation Coach, using the Dinky mould, was made by Marusan of Japan from about 1961 until 1964. It was part of a small range of diecast toys, generally based on items from the Dinky range.

It was supplied in a livery of sky blue with a dark blue flash together with polished metal rather than cast wheels which were used by Dinky. Another difference was the upper front windows, which were much larger on the Japanese variant. The difference can be clearly seen when comparing both examples side by side.

Dinky

Marusan

The presentation box described it as an 'Avenue Bus'. It is a rare toy to find nowadays.

Double Deck Bus:

1. Handmade larger copy of the Dinky double deck bus
2. Tinplate version made in Japan, possibly by the company Shioji, *deduced from the letters SSS and a lion motif on the box that this toy came in*
3. An actual Dinky Double Deck Bus for comparison.

A copy by Somerville. Over the years Somerville have produced a variety of high quality handmade models.

Despite its appearance the heavy weight of this toy is proof that it's not a real Dinky.

A combination of an early post war chassis with a late production body with the enlarged front windows.

The Dinky Toys Collectors Association

The Dinky Toys Collectors Association exists for those interested in Dinky Toys of all shapes and sizes. Above are two replicas from the original range:

- The number **75** on the Streamlined Coach is to 'celebrate' the 75th anniversary of the start of the Dinky Toy range. There were 250 made

    The box has an image of the toy and indicates the Associations origins, 2003 – 2009.

- In 2013, the copy of the 29A was one of 100 produced to commemorate the 10th anniversary of the Dinky Toys Collectors Association

A variety of modern copies of four different transport vehicles made by Dinky over the years.

They are sold unpainted, but can be bought painted.

The Morestone Bus

The Morestone name originated from the names of two people who had started a business selling toys. They were Sam Morris and Mr Stone, the latter not playing any part in the running of the business. Harry Morris joined his brother in the business. The company was called Morris & Stone and the Morestone label was used as a promotional name. They bought many of their early products from a company called Modern Products, but later setup their own manufacturing facilities. In 1959, Morestone became the Budgie range of popular toys, with Modern Products continuing to supply some of their items.

The livery was generally red with adverts: 'Finest Petrol Esso in the World'; 'Esso for Happy Motoring and the rarer 'Motor Oil Esso Petrol'. This latter advert was normally found on the Morestone Foden Petrol Tanker that was built from 1955 to 1957.

Their green toy has only been seen with the advert 'Finest Petrol Esso in the World'.

The Morestone Double Deck Bus first appeared in 1955 with production lasting until 1958.

It's seen as a copy of the Dinky 290 bus, but with some subtle differences:
- number '7' cast on the front destination screen
- deeper windows, than Dinky, on all sides
- looks chunkier
- 'Made in England' on the chassis

When comparing the Morestone copy with the Dinky, it is taller because of the way the chassis has been set on the wheels.

A real Dinky for comparison

The box is similar in style to Dinky's with an artist's impression of the bus with the advert 'Finest Petrol Esso in the World' on the sides. 'Morestone' and 'Double Decker Bus' are on all sides of the box.

The Metosul Bus

The company started in Espinho, a town located not far from Oporto in Portugal, by the owners Luso Celuloida de Henriques & Irmao Lda. Founded by brothers Manuel and Arthur Henriques. The company originally made plastic door handles and other fittings. To take up slack they started to produce plastic toys, eventually moving over to the production of diecast toys. It is believed that production of diecast started in 1963, with the manufacturing company choosing to discontinue toy making in 1989.

The name Metosul originated from 'Luso' reversed to 'Osul' and prefixed by 'Met' to distinguish the metal toys from the plastic series.

Metosul added a left-hand drive double-deck Leyland Atlantean bus to its range. This was a good copy of the Dinky Leyland Atlantean. It is believed that it was introduced in the late 1960's, with the possibility of the registration number of 1968 being an indication of its year of release. The Dinky casting it was based on had the entrance switched to the other side and the rear bustle was altered. The original casting being the rare variant with the single front entrance door.

Known colour schemes and fleetnames were: for Carris red/cream, green/cream and blue/white/red; for STCP green/cream; for SMC (black lettering) yellow/white; for Transul (white lettering) maroon/grey - sometimes without a fleetname. Also there is an all cream toy in a shade deeper than on the standard issue and without a fleetname.
Interior seat colours varied and included gold, brown, blue and two different shades of yellow.

First Casting

Second Casting

The casting was further altered with:
- double wheels replaced single wheels on the rear axle
- the front destination screen moved to above the windscreen and the rear one being removed
- new vents were cast in the roof to replace the front and rear vents
- a Leyland badge was added to the front of the vehicle

It was an exact replica of the Dinky toy in regard to size, hence the company must have put a lot of effort into making it work. Over the years it was produced, about 40 variants were made by Metosul.

35 Autocarro Leyland Atlantean TRANSUL
33 Autocarro Leyland Atlantean S.T.C.P.
23 Autocarro Leyland Atlantean CARRIS
34 Autocarro Leyland Atlantean S.M.C.

The second casting had many liveries indicating it was in production for several years. Popular colour schemes and fleetnames were: for Carris green/cream, red/cream, orange/cream, blue/white/red (Gazcidla more unusual livery - two different shades of red); for SMC (lettering in red or black) yellow/white; for Transul (revised lettering in either yellow or gold) red/grey or red/white; for STCP orange/cream (but different shades to Carris version).

Slightly rarer liveries: for Carris khaki, brown/cream, blue/cream, blue with a cream band; for SMC orange/white, green/white, yellow/grey; for TAP grey (2 different shades) having a white roof and lower panel with a red stripe and TAP along its sides; for CI green/cream.

There are at least eight different colours for the interior seats.

This toy was available with or without adverts. It is very difficult to tie many of the adverts down to a specific livery, because they were put on the models in the factory and in any order. Also the models were sometimes sold with separate adverts you could put on yourself

Popular adverts: Fenistil, Vibrocil, Varecort, Venoruton, Sacor, Sonap, Mabor, Fina and Avis Alugamos Automoveis - Rent a Car.

Carris Gazcidla

Portuguese Airways on the sides of the grey variant.

131

A sample of the variety of liveries in which the model was produced.

First Casting

Second Casting - with the different style of lettering for Transul

133

First Casting

Second Casting
S.M.C in different colours

Various liveries of the second casting demonstrating:
- colour variants
- interior seating differences

A Metosul Catalogue

LEYLAND ATLANTEAN
33 STCP, 34 SMC, 35 Transul

LEYLAND ATLANTEAN
36 GAZCIDLA, 44 STCP, 45 Carris

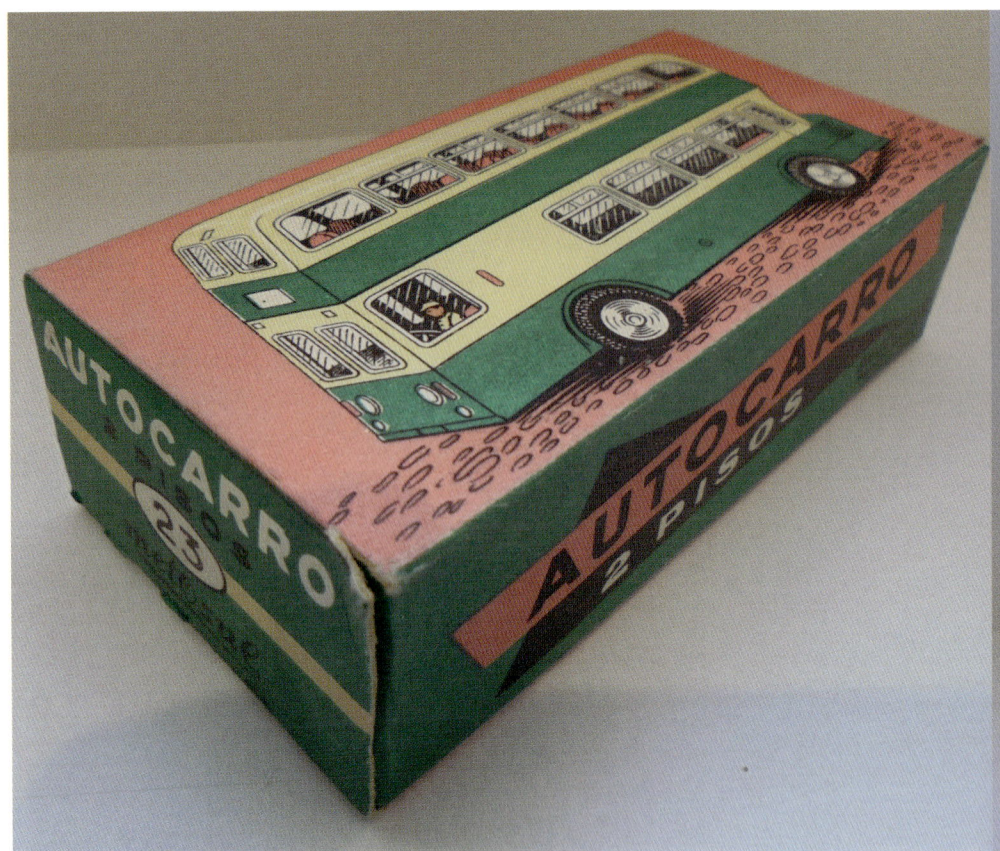

The first box used was green and pink with a yellow strip on the end flaps that displayed the catalogue number 23. There was a line drawing of the green/cream toy along the sides. This box usually contains the first casting of the model, but this is not guaranteed.

The yellow replacement box came with a window enabling the specific Leyland Atlantean toy to be seen. The appropriate catalogue number was either printed or stuck on the end flap.
There are two distinctive shades of yellow to look out for. Sometimes for special issues like the TAP, an appropriate sticker is found on the side of the box. Only one promotional box has been seen, this being for Varecort in green and silver, with all the writing in blue.

Autocarro 2 Pisos translation is Double Decker bus.

Thanks to D. Wallace for his help with the original article on Metosul

Metosul Adverts

Real Life Operators in Portugal with Fleetnames explained

- STCP - Societa de Transport Collective de Porto, which was based in Porto. It was also known as Oporto Tramways
- Carris was the main operator in Lisbon
- Transul was a provincial bus operator
- SMC was a Coimbra undertaking
- TAP - Transportes Aereos Portugueses
- CI remains a mystery - *do you know perhaps?*
- Gazcidla used vehicles contracted from Carris. Gazcidla was a large public gas-producing utility based in Lisbon, who operated a service to carry its workers to and from the factory. The livery of their vehicles was more unusual being blue/white/red.

Many of these operators had bought buses which had been made in the UK, including a variety of double deckers of which there were many Leyland Atlanteans, with Caetano built Metro-Cammell style bodies.

STCP bought 130 of the real vehicle.

Photos courtesy of Vic Davey, taken during his trip to Portugal in 1992, showing that Carris also had a large fleet of Leyland Atlanteans.

Plastic Copies

Luxury Coach

Plastic copies of the Maudslay Luxury Coach were manufacturer in Hong Kong by Mak's, probably to a scale of about 1:50.

This toy has been seen in blue, red, yellow and green with or without interior detail.

Dinky toy

Earlier versions had colour flashes along the sides similar to those on the Dinky toy.

Dinky toy

The box shows a Luxury Coach travelling through a green countryside.

Double Deck Bus

This large plastic Double Deck Bus copy was made in what was then Yugoslavia. These could be bought well into the late 1980s.

They came in a variety of colour schemes that included: blue/yellow; grey/orange and yellow/white. Reverse liveries were possibly also available.

A version was seen containing sweets with the upper deck having a lift-off lid.

A Dinky 290 is positioned next to the copy for size comparison.

Photograph by D Wallace.

Streamlined Bus:
1. An original Dinky version
2. A copy made of resin. Only a few were available for the collectors market

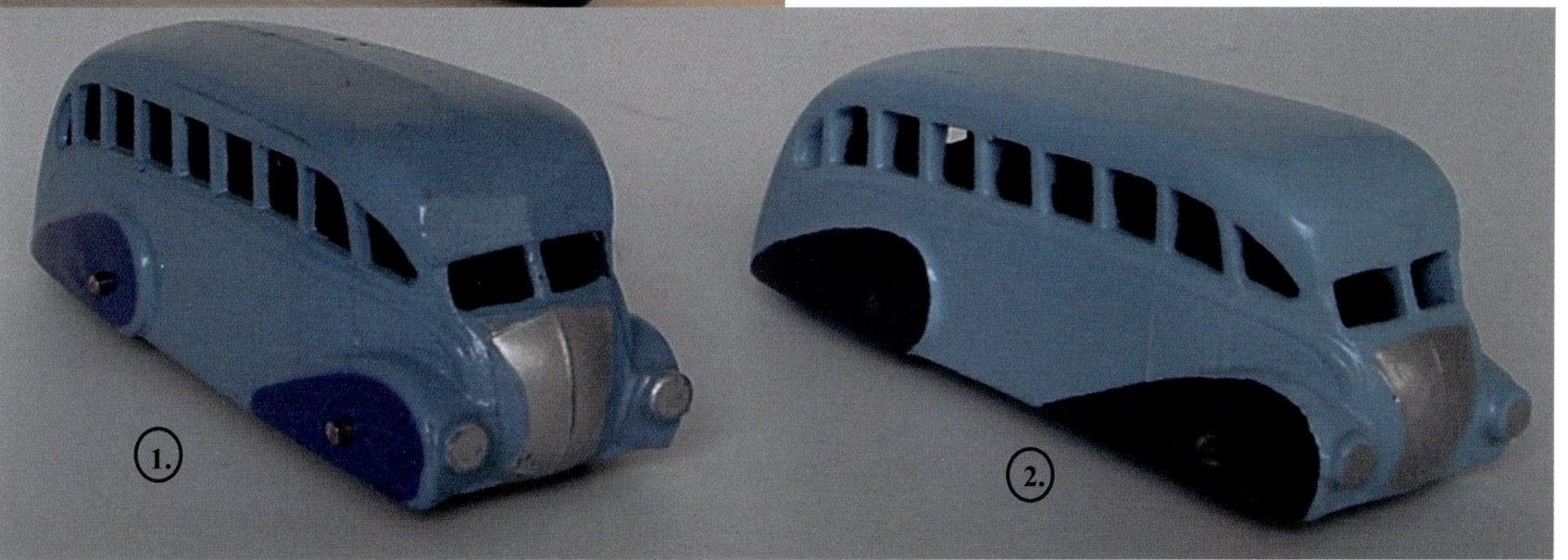

Duple Roadmaster Coach

There are a number of copies of the Duple Roadmaster Coach. An unusual one is Kemplas by Industria Argentina. Maybe the 'copy' idea does not apply because this plastic toy was made in the 1950's and based on vehicles then operating in South America. Which poses the interesting question, "who copied whom?"
"Were Duple and Dinky copying the South American vehicle?"
The Kemplas is identical in design & colour to the Dinky.

Kemplas

Other copies found are much smaller than the Dinky toy.

From New Zealand cereal packet

Dinky toy

An almost perfect copy possibly used on a board game as it's N gauge in scale.

New Zealand cereal packets copies photographed in front of their Dinky equivalent
Photographs D Wallace.

140

Routemaster Bus

The most iconic London bus is the AEC Routemaster and many have been copied in metal and plastic.
Only a small selection are shown here.

It can clearly be seen they are copies of the original Dinky toy.

The four shown here were made to a slightly larger scale than the Dinky toy.

Even the window bars have been included, so an earlier Dinky Routemaster was copied.

These models were made to the scale of 1:50 and were generally available via a variety of outlets.

On occasions a special run would be commissioned for a company, as was the case with WH Smith.

Wayne School Bus

A shortened copy of the Wayne School Bus was made in Hong Kong in a variety of colours.

It was available with either a push and go friction drive or with poseable steering driven by a battery motor.

Photographs by D Wallace

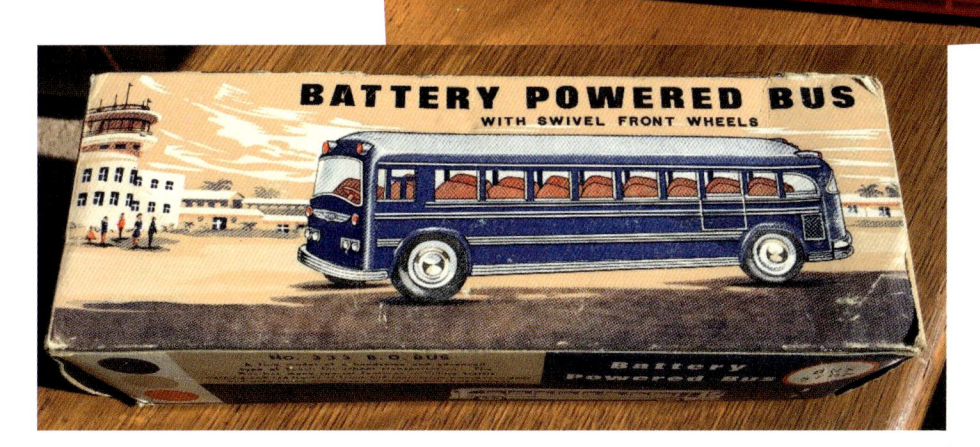

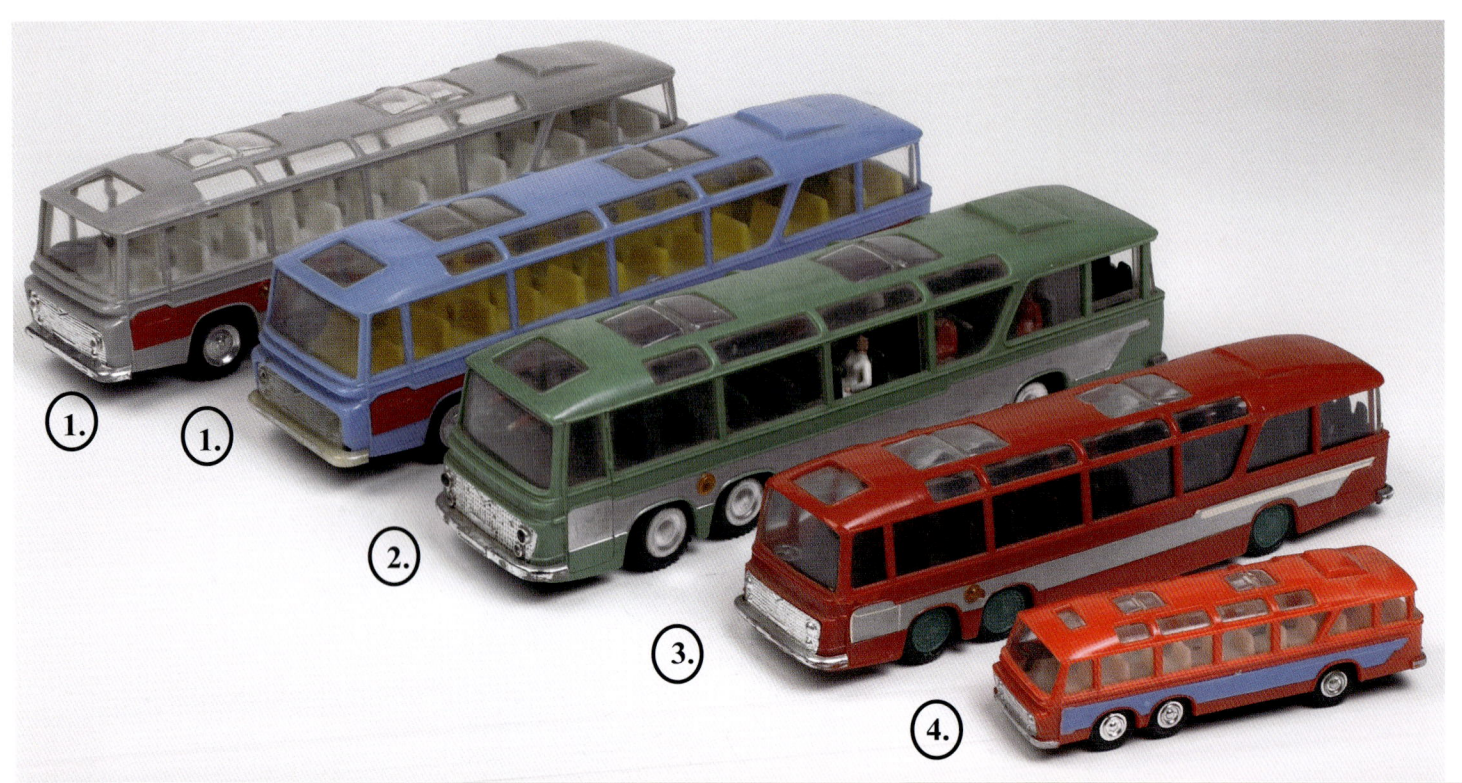

Vega Major Luxury Coach

The Vega Major Luxury Coach was one of the most copied of all the Dinky diecast models being made at the time. Countless plastic versions were made by manufacturers in Hong Kong, who seemed to be replacing Japan as a major toy manufacturing country.

The copies come in many sizes:
1. NFIC
2. Lucky on chassis, Telsalda on box - is the same size as the Dinky and initially included flashing lights powered by a battery, opening features, and even passengers
3. ROXY on chassis, Clifford Toys on box
4. Laurie Toys manufactured the smallest ones

NFIC with left-hand drive

The NFIC Cragstan toy was later copied in China and was being produced until recently.

ROXY on chassis

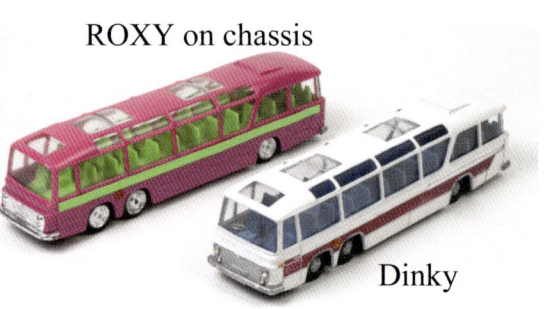

Laurie Toys

Dinky

This NFIC toy is rare as it wasn't made for the home market because it's a left-hand drive.

NFIC

Leyland Atlantean

The Leyland Atlantean model was also copied many times. Most of which were based on either a 1:76 or a 1:50 scale. They were sold in souvenir shops around the World and described as a "Typical British Bus"

The majority were made in Hong Kong by companies such as NFIC and Blue Box.

NFIC made the largest plastic model. It was produced in the red/white livery and had an opening engine bonnet

Blue Box made an almost exact copy of the Leyland Atlantean in vacuumed chromed plating and red.

Dinky original

Other manufacturers are in Sri Lanka (Ceylon - Palicrafts/ C V Bhatt).

Blue Box from Hong Kong

NFIC

Hong Kong

Hong Kong

No 11
Hong Kong

NFIC

NFIC made the toy in a variety of sizes and for special events like the Expo 86 in Vancouver.

NFIC

Made in Hong Kong for Telsalda

Made in China

BOAC Coach

Several copies of the BOAC Coach were made in plastic and manufactured in Hong Kong:

1. The Mak's BOAC was an accurate copy of the Dinky model. Early ones were supplied with interior seating detail. Its box promoted it as a BOAC Coach, with a clear image of an English cathedral in the background. Later Mak's versions were produced in various single colours, including yellow, light blue and red, sometimes with a white upper body. There were a variety of box designs for the non BOAC variants

2. A copy of the Mak's single colour version

3. A slightly larger version was produced with a different front end. It was a remote control variant and for that reason its box was much larger than normal. It was supplied with interior seating detail. The maker is unknown because no name appear on either the toy bus or the presentation box

4. Dinky original

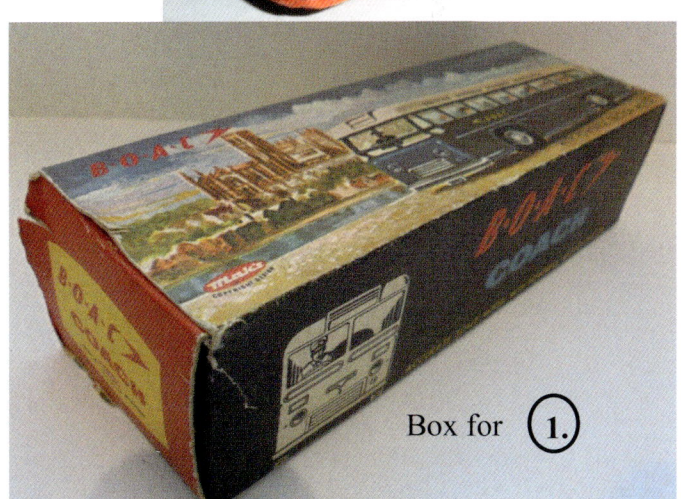

Box for ③

Box for ①

147

Dinky toy

Single Deck Bus

A large plastic copy of the Dinky Single Deck Bus was made by NFIC, in Hong Kong, with catalogue number 3107. Like the Dinky it even included the button on the side to open the doors. It was supplied in a lift-off box featuring great artwork which is almost something of a collectors' item in its own right.

Later versions, produced in China, appeared in a variety of colours, many with School Bus stickers.

Atlantean City Bus

1. Early versions of the Lincoln International toys have interior details, a well-balanced shape and were fitted with a friction driven motor. The name 'Lincoln' appears on the advertisements as well as on the base. The destination states '12 Wembley'.
2. In 1977, Lincoln International produced a Silver Jubilee variant with a friction driven motor.
3. Later toy with a compartment to insert a battery. The front wheels turn. Destination '12 Wembley'. No mention of the manufacturer.
    - more recent examples from China have a clear plastic upper deck.
    - a single-deck version was also made, but is difficult to find nowadays.

4. Exact replica of the Dinky. Manufactured in red with a chassis that is fixed with a screw. The doors and lights are painted in silver, the interior on both decks is cream, the route number is 221 and destination is 'Kings Cross'. It was supplied with promotional advertisements announcing 'Welcome to London'.
5. Later and slightly cheaper versions can be found in red and green, with the lower interior seats in the colour of the bus and the upper deck seats being cream. Doors and lights are no longer painted silver. Examples here of advertisement 'Welcome to Dublin'. Route number is 29 and destination is ATA Cliathe.
6. Made to a similar scale as the Dinky, though a little too large in width, carries advertisements for 'TK Toys' and is supplied with interior detail and a driver.

Manufactured by:

1. Popular Plastics Ltd, a UK based company
2. Lincoln International
3. *Unknown* but made in Hong Kong

Dinky original

Over the years, Dinky produced a few models in plastic for a variety of reasons:
- to offer a cheaper product
- to test reactions from future buyers
- as colour samples

The most famous is Thunderbird 2, but there are others which included the Blaw Knox Bulldozer.

These 3 toys were bought many years ago. They all have Dinky chassis' and their body is similar to the Dinky original.
Who made them?
Are they original Dinkys?